From Impossible to I'm Possible

Martin E. Folan

Kind acknowledgment is made for permission to reprint the following: "Night Prayer" from *A Catholic Prayer Book* (Our Sunday Visitor) by Fr. Robert J. Fox, copyright 1974, with permission of the copyright owner.

Scripture quotations taken from "Good News for Modern Man" *The New Testament* in Today's English Version (American Bible Society), New York.

A few names in this story were changed.

ISBN Number 1-57087-416-6
Library of Congress Catalog Card Number 98-66936

Professional Press
Chapel Hill, NC 27515-4371

Manufactured in the United States of America
99 00 01 02 03   10 9 8 7 6 5 4 3 2 1

Preface

An unexpected, paralyzing accident challenges the faith and courage of even the most "put together," mature woman or man. But for a seventeen-year-old young man, the shock of the loss of mobility, of memory, of being able to think and speak clearly, agonizes to the point of despair.

Marty Folan, sixteen years after his bicycle accident, describes in honest, vivid detail his journey back to health...physical, emotional and spiritual. From despair to hope, from fear and anger to joy, from loss to a renewed sense of the giftedness of all of life. So does Marty pen his saga.

The dialogue Marty recalls with his family— encouraging, challenging with honesty and consoling—captures the nuances of words and feelings for those of us who know his parents and sisters.

One recurring theme echoes through the narrative: the significance, for Marty, of deepening his ability as a long distance runner. This awareness of what was, for him, a peak life experience, also deepened his awareness of himself as someone able, meaningful and connected. This self-understanding of being a long distance runner also connected with the day-by-day, month-by-month struggle Marty endured.

Most young people will not be challenged as profoundly as was Marty. There are many other setbacks, disappointments, losses and rejections that youngsters—and all of us as well—endure. Perhaps Marty's abiding trust in God's immediate, caring presence—obscure, hidden, but nonetheless real—perhaps Marty's heroic, honest struggle will inspire readers to know that if they "hang in" and hold on, they, too, with the power of the Spirit, will overcome.

(Rev.) George J. Kane
July 2, 1998

Prologue

Some psychologists say that the earliest memories in one's life become a theme throughout that person's lifetime. Earliest memories in most people date back to when they were about 3 years old. Good or bad isn't the question as much as the content of the memory.

Topper the bouncing horse belonged to my older sister Cindy. A white horse with a black mane and red saddle, Topper hovered three feet above the carpet in Cindy's bedroom attached by four springs at each corner of a metal frame. Fascinated with the Lone Ranger, I donned my own black mask and hat and mounted Topper one Saturday afternoon.

"Hi-ho Silver, away!" I bounced high on the saddle and looked out over the imaginary horizon for oncoming Cherokee tribes. I rode alone across the rugged terrain. My mind at ease that no enemies were in sight, I assumed a rider's position upon the saddle, but ol' Topper cracked in half, split through the saddle, and hurled me onto the ground.

The sound of a fractured plastic horse, a small cowboy's body tumbling to the ground, and successive wailing beckoned chief marshal Daddy to the scene.

"What happened?" he asked in wonderment. "It looks like there's been a shoot-out at the corral in here." He observed the two horse halves on the ground next to my hat, springs detached from the frame and my little face wet with tears. He picked me up in his arms and carried me into the kitchen for a frosty mug of root beer.

Memory number one, an accident.

The rest of my childhood was relatively unsafe as well.

◆　　　◆　　　◆

"C'mon, kids! Daddy's got the pool set up," Mom called out to my sisters, Jeannette and Cindy, and me one Saturday afternoon in my second grade year. A pretty big pool for a kid my size, all of three feet deep and five feet across. I would've drowned had it been any bigger. I couldn't swim.

Inflatable life preservers, scuba masks and I became family in the water. They helped me become more acclimated to water in the oceanic backyard resort.

Then, on a calm Sunday afternoon with the thermometer resting between 80 and 90 degrees, and lifeguard Daddy on a 10-minute break inside the house, a scene predating Peter Benchley's "Jaws" rocked the Folan household.

Either its teeth were as sharp as Jaws' or an unkind fish hadn't manicured its nails, but whatever Sabertooth fiend dwelled at the depth of our 3-foot-deep pool, it had sunk its chompers into my kneecap and sliced my leg open. Blood rushed out into the pool and turned it into a biblical Red Sea. I screamed for help.

Either paralyzed with fear that his son's life was in jeopardy, or horrified at the sight of blood, Dad rushed to the scene of the calamity and prayed.

"Oh, Jesus!" he called out whenever peril had befallen one of his children. "What happened?"

Brought into the bathroom for medical treatment, I told Dr. Dad the truth. "A shark or a fish with very sharp teeth bit my knee and it started bleeding all over."

To this day, a two-and-one-half inch shark bite scars my right knee.

Within months, the first of a series of head contusions occurred while I walked through an outdoor shopping mall with my family. Several yards ahead of my parents, I strode aimlessly headfirst into a light post. "Ouch!"

"Oh, honey, are you okay?" Mom rushed to my side and rubbed my head.

"You got to watch where you're going, Mart," primary educator Dad advised me.

◆　　　◆　　　◆

"He needs glasses," the eye doctor told Mom and Dad next week after an appointment. I knew it going in. Dr. Dad had provided a pre-exam in the Folan family room a few days earlier. Seated on the floor in front of the couch, he stood across the room and held up the front page of a newspaper and covered all but the largest letter.

"Can you read that?" he asked.

"Is that an 'O'?" I guessed.

"Not quite. That's a 'C'. Let's try another one," he said.

Three guesses in three attempts and I had struck out.

Spectacled two weeks later with Coke bottle lenses and much sharper eyesight, I became known as the "Little Professor."

◆　　◆　　◆

Next accident in line, head trauma number two.

"Mom, I'm going out front to play catch with Scott." It was August, the summer before fourth grade. Scott rode his sister's bicycle to my house, and we played catch with a football in the front yard. While I never fell behind academically, I was recreationally deficient. I couldn't swim, ice skate, hit a fast ball, or ride a bike.

"Scott, can I try and ride your bike?" I begged my friend for an opportunity to acquire the skill of most elementary schoolers.

"Sure, go ahead, but it's my sister's bike," he said.

I had mastered the purple two-wheeler with training wheels, but hadn't yet learned to balance myself and shift my weight on two wheels.

Nervous, I hopped on and peddled the light yellow girls 10-speed bike. Shaky, I stopped and started a half dozen times on the sidewalk. I was afraid to ride any faster for fear that I might fall. Two consecutive houses

I'd maintained my balance, and now for the turn around in the apron of a driveway and...BAM! I'd fallen off the bike and smashed my head on the concrete. Blackout.

◆　　◆　　◆

Next I knew, I was at the bottom of my parents' driveway, holding my head, unaware of what had happened. As I walked through the doorway into the house, Mom was talking with our next-door neighbor, Mrs. Fitzgibbon.

"What's the matter, Mart?"

"Nothing, I'm just tired," I said, then walked into my bedroom and lay down.

Scott followed me in.

"Mrs. Folan, Marty was riding my sister's bike and he fell off and hit his head," Scott reported.

A trip to the hospital confirmed Mom's suspicions: a fractured skull.

Thereafter, minor bumps and slight bruises, scratches and a broken thumb sophomore year during football began to debunk the theory that one's earliest memory of life becomes thematic. The summer after eighth-grade graduation, Dad and I began to nail the coffin shut on any such theory with our own plan of action: conditioning.

"Mart, I played football for four years at St. George and one thing the coaches always emphasized was physical conditioning," he lectured me at our first training session.

"Our head coach said, 'If you guys are going to win, you've got to play harder than your opponents. You've got to hit harder, outrun them, outmuscle them, outthink them and outscore them. And you can only do all that if you are in condition.'"

"Mart, he was right," Dad said, as he stretched out his legs for a run with me.

Dad never liked to run. I knew that. Sure, he played high school football, served in the Air Force, tried to play tennis and currently plays 16-inch softball. Those were competitive sports played with equipment. Scores were kept but running wasn't that important.

As a corollary to his theory that running, in and of itself, seemed senseless, he postulated that as a means by which a greater end was being served, running was thereby deemed purposeful.

"We'll take two laps around the field and see how we feel after that," he said, looking out at the vast expanse of land behind the house.

Halfway through the first lap, I was already in a groove. Steady and smooth pace. Breathing easy. Feeling strong. "How you doing, Mart?" he asked, panting and puffing hard.

"This feels good, Dad," I said. "In fact, I'm beginning to like this."

A step and a half ahead of Dad, I felt a surge of energy and picked up the pace. Dad lagged behind. "Hey, Mart," he called out, "don't increase your speed too much and overwork yourself. You want to build up to it. This is only your first time out."

I didn't know it then. In fact, it wasn't until years afterward that I realized running would not only serve as a means of conditioning for football, but for life as well.

Sometimes we never understand why things happen in life. Quite often, there is no reason. But there will come a time when a light will shine, and if you choose to follow it, and live through the question, curses will magically transform into blessings and weaknesses will become strengths.

I dedicate this book to everyone who reads it and everyone who shined a light on me during my long journey.

Most of all, I dedicate this book to my Mom and Dad, sisters Jeannette and Cindy, and my best friend Rob. Without you, I would not have survived this journey.

I thank Jeannette and Cindy for their contributions to this book, because I know recalling such memories is still painful.

With Love,

Marty

Chapter 1

Beads of sweat rolled from the wrinkles on my forehead down my nose and into my eyes causing a sting I'd barely noticed. My concentration cut like a knife through the early morning heat, as I awaited the starting gun for the town's annual 10-kilometer race. Two hundred fifty runners packed in at the starting line with their adrenaline pumping so hard you'd swear the town was about to explode. Women and men from their teens up to mid fifties, dressed in crotch-high shorts and halter tops and T-shirts, some with Walkman radios, others with runners' wristwatches, and still more runners with so much gear on I'd swear they were packing for a safari.

This was my race. I'd trained diligently for one year. Seven days a week I'd squatted sets of ten, then twenty-five, then fifty. I'd run six days a week as hard and fast as humanly possible, finishing every run completely exhausted to ensure myself I'd trained as hard as possible that day.

I'd played tennis, softball and basketball seven days a week. My best friend Rob and I would take long bike rides. And now at five-foot, ten inches tall, my legs could rocket me high into the air so I could slam-dunk a basketball. I felt superhuman.

Was there more to life than running? I wondered. As a seventeen year old, I doubted it, although a mysterious silver-lined cloud of belief hung over me. Maybe there was something more.

"BANG!" The gun shot off and a slingshot full of runners fired us all out into the streets of Hoffman Estates. Like a keg of dynamite, I exploded out front of most every runner and pumped my arms and legs to lengthen my lead. The mere anticipation of a race sets the body's central nervous system in high gear.

Fluid poured throughout my body, sweat seeped through my pores, blood pumped through my heart, and adrenaline rushed to propel my whole self forward in one motion. I experienced freedom. Henry Nelson Wieman, the great philosopher of creativity, defined freedom as, "the whole self in motion."

I wasn't running against anybody. Nobody was my competitor and everybody was part of my team. I raced to better my time against myself, whatever my time was in the previous race. Last summer, same race, I finished ninety-second in the same field, my time was forty-five minutes and two seconds. Pretty shoddy. Mediocre was my personal judgment of the run, and that reflected my perception of who I was, to everybody I knew. My running affected all parts of my life. The only ones who understood were those running beside me.

Greater camaraderie existed among runners than among athletes in any other sport I knew of. We were family.

"How's it going?" a tall, slender man with a black mustache pulled up alongside of me after the first half mile. He stayed with me for the next quarter.

"I haven't felt better," I spoke audibly, though breathing hard before outpacing him after our short race.

"Keep it up!" he shouted as I stepped up my pace.

"Five fifty-eight! Five fifty-nine! Six minutes!" the time-keeper shouted out to me as I sped past the first mile marker.

Excellent time, I thought. Keep it up, Marty. Keep it up. The fastest mile I'd ever run was last summer. A five-minute, seventeen-second mile, and that was at the track at high school, not in a 6.2-mile race. But a first mile time of five fifty-eight promised me a personal record for the 10km run.

Stop thinking about the finish. Concentrate on this mile and your breathing. Inhale, stride, stride, stride, exhale. Pump those arms, head up, shoulders back, don't slump. Your breathing, arm movement, steps and concentration on the road are all happening at once. Perfect synchronicity. All one movement.

My second conscience-guide perched himself on my shoulder and observed me throughout my run. Prior to his appearance, I had learned to listen to myself, or what I thought was myself. My mind. My body. My inner spirit. It was only then that I realized a guide actually existed and that the voice I'd heard wasn't a figment of my imagination. Seven months ago, I'd begun logging the days' events, my personal thoughts, reflections and feelings in a journal. From those pages packed with stories of my successes and failures, aspirations, hopes and desires and people meetings, a second Marty arose. A protector against repeated mistakes, second Marty would shout loudly to me whenever I'd arrived at a point where he deemed his guidance worthy of my heeding.

"Jogged two and a half miles to school before setting personal best time in mile, five minutes, seventeen seconds," I'd written in the journal a year ago. "I think it helps to warm up and jog a distance before running a race. It prepares me physiologically and psychologically. Remember, jog before racing."

And that makes perfect sense! Who doesn't practice and train before any major performance? Athletes, musicians, actors, even moms and dads must discipline themselves before performing their greatest feats, as do the world's greatest basketball players like Kareem Abdul-Jabbar, or composers like Beethoven. Or even my parents.

"Go, Marty, great running! Keep up the pace!" my friend Mike Felten shouted from the curb in front of his house as I ran by. Mr. and Mrs. Felten smiled and waved at me as well.

I don't know why he doesn't take up running. He's a strong forward in basketball and our best hitter on the church softball team. He's tall and lean, I think he'd benefit from running distances. I'll talk to him about it.

"Eleven forty-eight! Eleven forty-nine!" I heard as I passed the second mile marker. I had improved the pace by about twelve seconds.

Outstanding, but don't speed up anymore. Burnout likely if pace continues. Steady. Lungs feel clean, air good. Not breathing heavy. Legs feel like the strongest part of me. Concentrate on arm and leg movements. Eyes on the next step ahead. Don't look up.

Only four runners were ahead of me. I maintained my pace behind them and didn't close the gap.

I wonder how long they've been running. They're about five years older than me, I estimated. Runners reach their peak sometime in their thirties, I've heard. Hmmmm, if I'm only seventeen and running as fast as I am and I keep up my training and conditioning, and eat a healthier diet, the good Lord only knows what my peak performance level will be. Nothing's going to stop me and there's no quitting.

One of the most exhilarating feelings I've ever had, running affected every aspect of my life. It set all parts in motion and with a certain rhythm that no other activity could make possible. My confidence reached astronomical levels. My thinking sharpened. Creativity flourished. Life seemed to have no limits. I felt one with everything in the universe.

I'd lengthened my lead to where I could hear nobody closing in behind me. I dared not look back, however. One of the universal principles of life, second Marty reminded me, is to keep your eyes sharpened on the route ahead of you and don't look back. Turning your head around and looking behind yourself breaks your concentration and takes precious seconds off your forward momentum. Looking back will hold you back.

"Seventeen fifty-eight! Seventeen fifty-nine!" I'd slowed down to a six-minute, ten-second third mile, which was still by far a personal best, but I didn't expect a twenty-second difference between miles. Geeze! I'd better maintain a more consistent pace.

I remember my first time out running, back when I was in eighth grade. Dad convinced me that if I wanted to play high school football, I'd have to get myself and my slender body into better physical condition. So he took me out back behind the house where the junior high school field was and jogged with me. Probably the only time he's ever jogged in his life. He's never gone out with me again. He doesn't even like jogging. But it took just once to lock me in. Thanks, Dad. I love it!

That's what everybody needs in life, not to run, but to find that one thing they can give themselves to completely, that will make them feel good about who they are and facilitate growth in all other areas of their life. Both Jeannette, 15, and Cindy, 19, found their one thing: music. There must be a musical gene on the female side of the family, because Mom is a gifted pianist and organist. Cindy and Jeannette are very gifted pianists, singers and songwriters. I hope they become great at it.

Footsteps closed in behind me, faster and faster they pounded.

*Don't let it impede your progress, Marty.
Continue at your own pace. Don't react to ex-
ternal elements. Steady and consistent. Inhale,
stride, stride, exhale. Take yourself from where
you are and grow from there. You can't run any
faster than as fast as you're prepared to run this
day, second Marty continued.*

That's what I want to make sure of, that I perform up
to my potential today. How can I assure myself of that?
By giving my all every day so that it becomes natural, but
not only in running — in everything I do! Running is inter-
connected with everything I do in life. This is what I'm
best at. I want to run for the rest of my life. Maybe I
could compete in the Olympics. I'm sure that conditioning my body and training for races would demand every
breath and absolute, complete discipline, but I know I
could do it. At least I could make the commitment to
train for the Olympic tryouts. I've got so much going for
me. I'm young, healthy, eat a well-balanced diet, don't
smoke or drink or take drugs. I'm a good student and
have a pretty good attitude about myself and running.
What else do I need but to focus on my goal and find a
coach?

"Twenty-four minutes, fifteen seconds!" I heard passing the four-mile marker. A six-minute, seventeen-second
fourth mile. Slowed down considerably from the first three,
but still satisfactory.

I knew I hadn't run this fast before. I was beside
myself with amazement. This was a self-transcendent experience for me, and here I was a seventeen year old in

high school. I thought only people like monks and the pope had self-transcendent experiences. And they probably don't even run!

I'll bet it's that God stuff that helps them. But how do they do it? Do they just get up at sunrise each morning, chant when they walk downstairs on their way to breakfast and contemplate life when they do their gardening chores? How does that make them godly people? Eh, maybe they read the Bible more thoroughly or say more prayers. But how do they know God really hears them when they pray? It's not as if they can pick up a phone and call Him on God-hotline. I go to church on Sunday mornings, and Thanksgiving, Christmas, Good Friday, Easter and holy days, but that's because I'm Catholic. I don't understand any more than that. It's a mystery to me.

I'd lost my concentration on running and found myself already at the five-mile mark: "Thirty minutes, forty-five seconds!"

Thinking about the God stuff is powerful. I never thought about it before, maybe because I don't understand it. How can you make sense of something you don't understand? Life is a lot like that, too. I'm only seventeen, though, so I guess it will all make sense when I get older.

I wonder what it's like to be a monk, or a hermit, who lives life all alone.

◆   ◆   ◆

As I headed near the sixth mile, the crowd cheered louder. I had dropped back behind a dozen runners. Several had overtaken me past the halfway mark, but I maintained my pace, without breaking stride. That didn't matter. I wasn't out to beat them, but only to improve my performance and run as fast as possible with their assistance. A couple hundred runners behind me sent a wave of energy up my spine and commandeered my charge right up to the finish line: "Thirty-eight, eighteen!" Finished.

Yessssss! A personal best time! Fifteenth out of two hundred fifty runners and second in my age group.

My body tingled with ecstasy, like a zillion tiny pins lightly piercing my skin from the inside. I was radiant with joy.

I had never imagined the possibility of running so fast a time, let alone finishing out in front of so many others. My future as a runner has no limits. Anything is possible. All I have to do is continue running, discipline myself, find a professional coach or trainer, keep the spirit and go, go, go!

"Hey, guy, great running," another runner congratulated me. "I saw you kicking in on the final stretch and thought you were going to catch up to me."

"Good legs, man," a short runner patted me on the back.

I walked over to the table for a cup of water and a banana and talked with a few other runners. When runners cross the finish line, it's like a family reunion. We're all part of the same family. We all share the same experience. Unity.

◆   ◆   ◆

I took the next week off from running, but continued lifting and playing softball, basketball, tennis and biking.

Friday afternoon, I ventured out on my bicycle in the blazing hot summer heat, with the mercury hovering over the ninety-five degree mark, and pedaled my shiny green three-speed bicycle down to my best friend Rob's house. A church softball game was scheduled for later in the evening. Co-captains, Rob and I took our team to the championship and won it the past two years. We anticipated capturing a third consecutive crown, but Jan Swadinski's team posed the biggest threat. They led us in the conference by two games and bulked the heart of their lineup with three muscular linemen from Schaumburg High School's football team.

Despite the odds being against us, I was confident we'd beat the pants off them. We'd won every game we played when the odds were against us. Why should tonight be any different?

As I rounded the turn off Berkley Lane, I saw Rob in his cutoffs and tank top mowing the lawn. I shouted across the yard. We had been friends since freshman year. A beanstalk with long arms and legs, Rob stood over me by about an inch, but I could outjump him on the basketball court. I got off my bike, walked over to him and slapped him a high-five.

"Let's go for one of our bike rides. We can talk about the game and who we want to put in at clean-up. Lazar hasn't been pounding the ball out these past few games like he used to for us, so we need someone who can give us that big punch when we need it."

Rob turned off the lawn mower and looked down with a grimace on his face. "I'm sorry, Mart, but I can't go for a bike ride with you. I just started this and my Mom said I need to have the entire yard cut before I play ball because the Grahams are coming over tonight," he said, with respect for his parents but well on the way to becoming his own person.

"Okay, I understand, but who should we put in at clean-up tonight?"

"Try Mike Felten," he said, mimicking the third-baseman's swing. "He's got such a smooth swing, and he's been a fairly consistent hitter. But listen, Mart, I have to get back to cutting the lawn. You make up the batting order and I'll see you there."

Back on the bike, I pedaled west to nowhere in particular and thought about my last year of high school up and coming.

Senior year, yes! Prom and post-prom. Senior breakfast. Senior ditch day. Graduation. Parties. College preparation. And finally, living on my own at a university. It only gets better from here, I assured myself.

Five miles down the road, I glanced to my right and saw a farmhouse across a field and a small pond nearby. Thirsty, I got off my bike and searched for a water pump.

"Well, hello there little fellah," I greeted the mid-sized black lab who ran over to welcome me and jumped up on his back legs to rest his front paws on my chest. "Say, I'm looking for a gulp or two of water. Do you know where I can find some?"

He seemed to understand me, but an armful of dog saliva was not quite what I had in mind.

I continued pedaling westward feeling as light as a bird soaring high above the clouds. Pedaling harder and faster, sweat rolled down my face. I spotted a gas station a hundred yards ahead.

"No shirt, no shoes, no service," the sign on the door read.

As long as they don't require identification, I'm okay, I thought, realizing my pocketless shorts had kept me from even carrying some change for an emergency candy bar, let alone my driver's license.

"Howdy," a short, fat, mustached man welcomed me. "What can I do for you, buddy?"

"I'm just out on a bike ride and kinda thirsty. Wondering if you could spare me a cup of cold water?"

"Help yourself," he said, pointing to a large water dispenser to his right.

"And could you tell me where I am? I rode west from Hoffman Estates and wound up taking some turns and got lost."

"Out that way is where you came from. Hoffman Estates, Schaumburg and Hanover Park are over there," he said, "and if you keep going that-a-way, you'll hit Elgin."

Back on the bike, I headed to Elgin. I've got time. Heck, nobody will miss me if I'm gone for the afternoon.

I turned the corner once in town and passed the Elgin City Limits sign before heading downhill near Trout Lake Boulevard and Dunbar.

There isn't much traffic on the road ahead, so I'll just cruise around the corner and ride down the main road to see where I'm going.

As I neared the t-intersection, I noticed my brakes needed tightening when...SCREEEEEECHHHH!!!! CRASH!!!! BAM!!!

Chapter 2

"Officer, all I saw was his bike coming around the corner and before I could blink, I heard a loud bang and felt impact on the jeep, and I saw his body bounce off the side and fall onto the ground."

"Okay, ma'am. Calm down. Are you okay? You seem a bit shaken up."

"Yes, I'm all right. Did you call an ambulance?"

"Yes, ma'am, one will arrive shortly and we'll take him to Sherman Hospital."

"I work there. I'm a nurse."

"About how fast was he going on the bike?"

"He seemed to be coming downhill fast, I think, but it seemed like he was slowing down when he took the turn. I can't really say because it happened so fast. Officer, is he going to be all right?"

"We'll have to wait and see. Now, I see that there is a stop sign on the corner where he turned, but I'd guess his view of the sign was obstructed. Do you see the tree branches dangling in front of the sign?"

"Oh, yes. I didn't notice that until now. So you think he couldn't see the sign?"

"I don't know. I'm just speculating."

◆　　　◆　　　◆

"We've got a white male, approximately 15- to 17-years-old, whose name and identity are not known at this time, in the emergency room in a comatose state," doctors reported.

"The left femur is fractured. There's probable laceration or complete thrombosis of the mid-portion of the left superficial femoral artery secondary to a displaced fractured segment of the left femur. Also a severe secondary vassal spasm and comatose state secondary to head injury," doctors stated on report forms.

Translation: broken left leg; cracked pelvis; fractured collarbone; paralyzed left arm; and in a coma.

"Nurse, please keep close watch on the male patient in ICU2," a doctor said. "Hopefully it won't be too long before someone comes in and identifies him."

Chapter 3

"Cindy, where's Marty? It's time for dinner."

"I don't know. He's not out back on the tennis courts. Maybe he's down at Rob's. Do you want me to call down there?"

"Yes and tell him to come home because Dad is going to be taking the hamburgers off the grill soon."

◆　　◆　　◆

"Hello, Rob? This is Cindy. Is Marty there?"

"No. He came down here earlier and asked me if I wanted to go for a bike ride with him, but I told him I had to cut the lawn, so I'd see him at the softball game."

"What time did he ask you to go bike riding?"

"Oh, it must have been around one o'clock or so. If I see him I'll tell him to go home if you want."

"Yeah, thanks, because we're having dinner and he's not around. When I find him, I'll tell him to meet you at the game."

"Okay, thanks. Bye."

◆　　◆　　◆

"Mom, Rob said he went out bike riding around one o'clock, but he hasn't heard from him since. Rob said he's supposed to meet Marty at the softball game at church."

"Well, make some more calls around to see if you can find him, Cindy."

One half hour later.

"Where is he? He never takes off like this for so long without letting us know where he's going. Who all did you contact, Cindy?"

"I called Scott, Kevin, Mike and Mary, but they said he didn't stop by or call them, then I got his phone book and called every one of his friends who live in the area, but nobody's seen or heard from him."

"Come and have dinner then, and when he gets here I'll fix his hamburgers."

The sun hung on the edge of the horizon.

"Mom, Rob's here and he wants to talk with you," Cindy said.

"Hi, Mrs. Folan. Marty didn't show up at the softball game and everybody there was kind of worried, so I was thinking that maybe we should all get in a car and go driving around looking for him. I've got my car out front, so if you all want to come with me, I'll drive."

"Okay. Let me go get Marty's Dad and Jeannette."

◆   ◆   ◆

"Rob, where do you usually go when you guys go bike riding?" Jeannette asked, getting into the car.

"Nowhere in particular. We sometimes go wherever we can find a tennis court, which may be at Evergreen Park or over by church. I don't think he'd be out playing tennis anywhere, especially since he knew we had a softball game tonight. He probably just went out on a bike ride and maybe met someone, maybe an old friend or something, and got caught up talking with him and just forgot the time."

"I think something's wrong. He always calls us if he's going to be out anywhere, and I just have a funny feeling he's in trouble," Cindy said. "He knew his Dad was putting hamburgers on the grill tonight. And you know how much he loves burgers."

Hours passed. The moon beamed a brilliant white against a pitch-black sky.

"Do you think maybe we should call the police and report him as a missing person, Mr. Folan?"

"Not enough time has passed, Rob. I think a person must be missing at least twenty-four hours before he can be considered a missing person. But I think a telephone call to the Hoffman Estates Police Department would be a good idea. Maybe they'll have some information."

"I tell you what, Rob. Why don't you drop us off at home and we'll make a call to the police department, and as soon as we find out anything, we'll give you a call," Mom said.

"Okay. Don't worry what time it is, because I have a phone in my room. And besides, my parents are concerned, too."

The night hours crept by slowly. Nobody slept soundly, as the anticipation of a phone call from the police department kept everyone on edge. At dawn, the coffeepot perked and nerves frazzled at the house.

At 9 a.m., Officer Benson of the Hoffman Estates Police Department appeared at the door to file a missing person's report.

"Come on in, officer," Mom said as she opened the door. Cindy, Jeannette and Dad stood in the kitchen, their eyes red and filled with tears. Officer Benson asked to use the telephone to contact emergency rooms at local hospitals, then, he called back to the police station.

"Yeah, Chuck, this is Larry. Would you go back over to the front desk and get that note brought in Friday evening, about the accident?" he asked. "Sure, I'll wait."

"Officer, did someone find him?" Cindy asked, growing more worried.

"I don't know yet, but there's a note about an unidentified youth hit in Elgin Friday afternoon," he said as he jotted down information. "Thanks, Chuck. Bye.

"I'm going to call Sherman Hospital to check on this lead," he said, dialing the phone.

"Yes, this is the Hoffman Estates Police Department. I'm calling about an unidentified boy brought into the emergency ward yesterday. Could you give me a description of him?

"Male, about 16 years old, no identification, white terry cloth tank top, shorts, riding a green Murray bicycle..."

"Oh no! It's him, it's him!" Mom cried out. "I can't believe it. It's Marty. He's been in an accident!"

Family members drew close to one another. Cindy, Jeannette and Mom cried out loud. Dad embraced everyone, trying desperately to fight back his tears.

"From the description they gave, it sounds like they found him," Officer Benson said. "He is in the hospital and he is alive. That's all the information they have. I'll need someone to come to the hospital to identify him."

"Cindy," Dad began, "I think it would be a good idea for you to stay here in case of any phone calls. Mom, Jeannette and I will go to the hospital. I'll call Rob, because he'll want to come with us."

◆　　　◆　　　◆

"Hi, Mrs. Fitzgibbon. This is Cindy. They found Marty," she said, crying uncontrollably. "He's in Sherman Hospital in Elgin. He was in an accident. Mom, Dad, Jeannette and Rob went to identify him. Could you come over?"

Moments later. "Cindy, let's sit down. I know you're shaken up a bit," Mrs. Fitzgibbon said. "Are they a hundred percent sure it's Marty?"

"He didn't have any identification, but from the description of his clothes and bicycle, I'm certain it's him. They said he's alive, but we don't know any more right now. Dad told me to stay here and wait in case anyone calls.

"Excuse me a minute, Mrs. Fitzgibbon. I want to call Bob, my boyfriend. He told me to call when we found Marty."

Across the room, she picked up the phone. It was very warm because of the numerous calls coming in and going out. "Bob, they found Marty," she cried out. "He's in Sherman Hospital in Elgin. I don't know what happened to him, but he's been in an accident. Please come over."

◆　　◆　　◆

"The unidentified boy is in intensive care," the receptionist at Sherman Hospital said to Officer Benson.

"Okay, folks. Follow me down the hallway," the officer said, leading the four down a quiet, dark corridor.

Jeannette ran ahead of everybody and into the room on the right.

"Oh no! Mom, Dad, it's Marty!" she yelled out loud, as tears rushed from her eyes down her cheeks. She stood next to the bed. Rob, Mom and Dad rushed over to the bed. Loud crying echoed out of the room and down the hallway.

"My god, why?!! This isn't fair! Why did it have to happen to him?!! Please, please, please, Marty, wake up," Jeannette pleaded. They all stood around the bed and cried.

A high energy of tension, brittle nerves and frozen fear sliced through the quiet stillness.

Drowning in tears, they embraced Rob, waiting, hoping.

No response, not even a movement.

The doctor in ICU approached Mom and Dad. "Mr. and Mrs. Folan, would you step over here, please?

"Your son has been in a very bad accident. From the police report, we learned that he was coming around a corner on his bicycle in Elgin and he apparently didn't see an oncoming vehicle."

"Oh, no!" Mom cried out and buried her face against Dad's chest.

"He fractured his left femur, suffered a slight crack to his pelvis and broke his collarbone. He is in a coma now, and we won't know the extent of his brain damage until consciousness returns."

"Do you think he'll come out of the coma, doctor?" Dad asked.

"I can't say whether or not he will, but we are going to keep him under twenty-four-hour watch."

"You said you won't know how severe the brain damage is until he comes out of the coma, but can you tell us anything about what we might be able to expect, considering what he's been through?" Dad asked.

"No, I really can't say, Mr. Folan. Since he sustained a major blow to the head, he may be unable to recall the accident. I don't want to fill you with hope that he'll regain consciousness and everything will be the way it used to be. Then again, miracles have happened before."

Their faces flushed with fear, as they teetered on the edge of hopelessness.

◆　　◆　　◆

"I'll go call Cindy," Mom said shortly, walking out of ICU.

"Cindy, we're here at the hospital and we found Marty. He has a broken leg and a concussion," she said, sounding relieved. "Now listen, here's what I want you to do. Lock up the house and come with Mrs. Fitzgibbon or maybe Bob to the hospital. We'll see you when you get here."

Two minutes later at the house the phone rang again. "Hello," Cindy answered.

"Cin, it's me, Jeannette," she said, crying. "I'm calling you back because I know Mom just didn't want to scare you. Cindy, Marty is hurt real bad. You've got to get here. Mom doesn't know I'm calling you. They are calling Fr. George Kane, so please come."

Bob pulled up in the driveway and drove Cindy and Mrs. Fitzgibbon to the hospital.

> *I can't believe this is happening. My own dear baby brother. God, where are you in all of this? Please, please, help Marty. Help us all. Just this one time.*
>
> *Bob and I found ICU. He stayed outside in the lounge. As I entered the room, Dad came over and hugged me. His eyes were red. I could tell he was fighting to hold back tears and trying his best to keep all of us from breaking down.*

"Cin, it's a lot more serious than we thought," Dad said. "Mart is in a coma, and he's being carefully watched."

Fr. George had arrived and stood at the foot of the bed and said prayers. Rob and Cindy stood by.

"Rob, I never ever expected to see this life in such a fragile state," she said.

"Is this the prayer of last rites Fr. George is saying?" Rob asked.

*I had to grab onto Rob's arm in his jacket.
My legs would not hold me up, and I think my
heart was crying out so loudly that everyone
could hear. I had not really been that close to
Marty's best friend Rob, but together in that
moment we cried helplessly. It looked as though
Rob had aged 40 years. His eyes sank in eight
inches and his face turned white.*

*So young, one asks and begs God to fix the
broken. Naive but sincere details are offered: If
only You could help us this once, dear God.*

*We have to send up the brightest light pos-
sible and as many voices as possible so God will
hear us. We don't want to lose this life, dear
God. Please don't take Marty from us.*

I know in my heart God won't refuse us.

◆　　◆　　◆

The next day Fr. Greg Sakowicz from the Church of
the Holy Spirit was contacted, along with other family
members, friends, and neighbors. Fr. Greg came home
from Notre Dame University where he had been taking
summer courses. Aunt Hinkie and Uncle Eddie, too, had
driven out many miles. Others came from as far west as
Elgin to as far east as Chicago. Rob and his Mom remained with the family the entire day. Bob and his parents
gathered round the bed in ICU. A list was compiled of
who visited the hospital each day.

Day two passed. No signs of movement.

23

Rob knelt down beside the bed with Fr. Greg. Tears streamed from Rob's eyes.

"Marty, if you can hear me, please don't let go. Hold on and fight it. I know you can come through it, Mart," Rob cried. "Fr. Greg, can you do something?"

"Loving God, our source of hope, our source of joy, our destiny. We pray to You in faith and ask that You restore Marty to full health. May he rejoin his family and friends and find his peace in You. We ask this all through Christ our Lord. Amen."

"Do you think he'll recover, Fr. Greg?"

"Rob, Marty was in a very bad accident and it will probably take a long time for him to recover, but I think that in time, he will be okay."

◆　　◆　　◆

Bob drove Mom and me home to get the family phone book and make calls. My faith was shaken because I knew our light was fading on the way home. Mom was in the back seat of the car as we rode down route 58. Tears soaked her face, then soft murmurs, and then louder whimpers turned into anguished sobs that tore my heart to pieces.

I saw her curled up and crying so desperately that all hope perished from my world at the sight of her pain.

Day after day after day.

◆　　◆　　◆

Four days in a coma. Then, consciousness returned.

"Mom! Dad! Marty opened his eyes and he moved! He's okay!" Cindy cried out a joyful shout of relief as Mom, Dad, Jeannette and Rob rushed over to the bedside.

"Oh, Marty," Cindy cried as she wrapped her hands around my head and held me close, "we were so worried that we were going to lose you."

The first battle in a long war had been won.

Wheeled out of intensive care on the seventh day, I found a new home in the hospital. "Mr. and Mrs. Folan, we're putting Marty into a private room on the corner next to the nurses station. That way we'll be able to always keep our eye on him and we'll be right there if he should need anything," the head nurse said.

"Okay, thank you," Dad said.

"Listen, when you get your ride to work in the morning, I'll drive out here with Rob's Mom and stay with him for the day, then I'll come and pick you up at work, we'll have dinner, then you can come back and spend the evening with him here," Mom, the family taxi driver, told Dad.

Chapter 4

1'm a rock by a stream. I can't move. I'm just here. People come and see me. They touch me. They talk to me. I can hardly speak. I slur my words. They feed me. They hold my bottle when I pee. They change the TV station. They bring me presents. I'm not healing. I'm eroding.

Needles jammed into my arm. Ointment rubbed all over my body. Tubes hanging by my bed. Here I lie. Here I'll die.

"Mart, look what Rob's Mom brought you." Mom smiled as she walked into the room holding up a home-made pillow with sports figures and my name sewn on it.

"That's nice. Thank you," I said, forcing a smile at Mary Ann. "I like it."

"It's good he can talk now," she said to Mom, noting the improvement I'd made the first week.

"The nurse said it'll be just short sentences at first, but he'll be talking like he used to. In a few weeks they'll have him in with a speech therapist," Mom said.

Week one. Visitors came by dozens. Retrograde amnesia blocked my memory of the accident. But the dog by the lake. A flash of a moment. I remember that.

But here I am. In a hospital. In pain. Inside myself I cry. How long before therapy? I want to get better. I want the cast off now! I want to lift weights. I want to run again. Help me! Doctors get paid enough. Medical technology is advanced enough. Why must I suffer? Make my legs work again! I can't live with one arm. I can't even run.

I cursed in bed. Nobody could help. My arm felt heavy. Like I laid it in cement. I moved my right leg freely. My left leg felt mangled. Twisted like a pretzel inside. Pain shot up my pelvic region. Straight up to my shoulders. I gulped down pills to kill pain. Nothing helped.

"How do you feel, honey?" Mom whispered. "Is there anything I can get you?"

They raised me seventeen years. Fed me. Clothed me. Hugged me. Loved me. This too is their pain. They can't help.

Mom stood beside the bed. She could've been in Alaska. She seemed so far away.

Everybody seemed distant, physically. I was like a Pet Rock, but never pet.

"Marty." A football teammate from high school entered the room. "Hi. I just heard about what happened and I couldn't believe it. I was thinking to myself last week, 'Football is going to be starting soon and I know Marty will probably play jayvee or varsity this season.'"

I glanced at his face. I couldn't remember his name. Lineman on defense. Center on offense. Number 56.

Ashamed I couldn't remember his name. We weren't friends out of school. He always talked with me in the hallways. He stood next to me on the sidelines. Who could it be?

"...so I was talking to the head coach and he said he heard from the cross country coach that you were in the hospital. I thought to myself, 'Jeff, you've got to go see Marty. You guys played football together since freshman year and it'd be nice if you visited him.' I wanted to know whether we'd see you out on the field this year at all."

Jeff Boldt. Now I remember. "I don't know, Jeff," I told him, not lying to him or myself, but refusing to face the truth that it would probably be a long time before I'd even walk. "My leg is broken. Healing shouldn't take too long. But I can't move my left arm. I guess I'll miss summer practice. Maybe even the first few games."

"It sounds like you'll be out there this season anyway," he said, his supposition filling me with hope. Someone believed I'd come through.

He stood by my bedside. I wish he'd bang his head against mine. I wish he'd butt shoulders like at practice. I want to feel his presence. Everybody who comes acts like I'm a living corpse encased in a tomb. Most people don't touch me. Don't they know I need to feel their presence? I need to feel living life.

As I talked with him, I noticed his clothes. Bright orange shorts. Blue tank top. Indications that I was missing out on a hot, sun-bright day. One that I should be enjoying. But the stark white hospital environment reeked with cleanliness and sterility. It had clamped me in its grip and wouldn't let go. Cold metal bed rails beside me. Longer rails near the toilet. Metal wheels on the wheelchair. Men and women people-fixers suited in pure white healing gowns. Equipped with repair tools and problem detectors. I remember when the doctor placed the diaphragm of his stethoscope on my chest. The coldness on my skin, every nerve in my body tingled. I lay in bed, wakened every morning by Miss Nice Nurse in White. The same feelings pierced my senses. I felt frozen.

I'm not healing. I'm dying. All signs pointed down the long dark corridor.

So I devised a new plan of my own.

Later in the week, members of the Knights of Columbus from my Dad's council paid visits to me, showered me with apologies and prayers and tried to offer emotional support.

"Pssst, Joe. Come here a minute," I whispered to brother knight Palella, a short, gray-haired man with a soft heart and an appeal of kindness.

"Yeah, Marty. Is everything okay?" he asked in a return whisper.

"Joe, you have that little pickup truck, don't you?"

"Yeah, it's parked outside. Why?"

"Joe, you go outside and drive it around the back and meet me there. You see, that way I can sneak out of here and meet you down there and then you can get me out of here."

"Oh, Marty," he said, taking a step backward from the bed, surprised at my request. "I don't know if that would be a good idea. I'm not supposed to do that."

Somebody has to help me. I can't walk out of here on my own. They'd notice me.

A tall slender nurse with long, shiny black hair served me a feast for dinner: turkey, stuffing, mashed potatoes, green beans, hot buttered rolls and a side of cranberry, which I hated.

"Here's your dinner, Marty," she said, placing the tray of food on the end table in front of me. Her name tag read Linda.

"Thank you, Miss Linda. I didn't think I would get any turkey until Thanksgiving. Is there pumpkin pie with this?"

"I'm not sure, but I can check for you after you finish your meal," she obliged.

"If there isn't, can we go out to the pie shop for a slice?" I decided she'd be my accomplice on the escape.

"You'll be able to go out for pie when you're released," she said. "I'll make sure you get some kind of dessert."

That eliminated any chance to escape.

Frustrated, yet hungry as a horse, I devoured the feast along with the slice of pumpkin pie Miss Linda served, then lay back down in bed. I looked around the room. Dozens of cards of all colors bordered all three tables in the room. Roses, carnations and daisies emitted scents of nature's wonderland beyond the walls of confinement. Presents. Posters. Letters and other healing antidotes. But no people. My first time alone. Family and friends were downstairs. Nurses sat at their desks outside my room at the corner. I'm at the peak of isolation.

Loneliness activated my body signals. Nerves froze. Flesh felt iced. Fear enveloped me. Even my stomach. I felt a tidal wave rushing through me when...MMMMMBLEEEEECCCHHH!! I heaved up dinner all over the bedspread on my lap.

"Oh, Marty," Miss Linda rushed into the room from her watchpost station, "I'm sorry. Let me get something to clean that up with. Do you think you had too much to eat?"

"I don't know. I probably ate dinner too fast so I could get to dessert. That pie certainly was good, Miss Linda, " I said with a twinkle in my eye. "But we should go out for pie next time. I think I ate a bad piece."

She smiled. "As soon as you're discharged."

A heavy stench of vomit hung thick in the air above my bed. Miss Linda rolled several sheets of white paper towel around her hand and scooped up the wet brown clumps from the bedspread. "I'll bring you some new sheets and covers, Marty."

"Can you bring me something more to eat? I'm still hungry."

She cared for me like a mother. Food. Clean sheets. New dressing for my sutures. Pain relievers. Aspirin for headaches. Radio batteries. I became as dependent on her as a baby for its mother.

"As soon as I clean up this mess, I'll see what I can get for you," she said. "I know they stopped serving turkey dinner meals, though."

I laughed to myself. I barf, someone else cleans it up. I want more food, someone brings it to me. I ask, I receive. I wish getting out of here were that simple. But I certainly don't see anyone jumping to usher me through the doors into Mom's car.

"Marty, all that was there in the cafeteria was a hamburger and fries," she said, placing a tray in front of me with packets of ketchup, mustard and relish, a plate of onions and tomatoes and a Coke. I was particular about my soda selection, especially nowadays, during the onset of cola wars.

"Hamburgers are my favorite. Thank you, Miss Linda."

As I looked over my mini-meal, I again felt like a king. Whatever I want, I get. At my weakest and most troublesome time in life, yet I'm cared for like a king. Is this what's meant by, "...and the last shall be first?" I am last. In fact, I'm lost.

I can't stand being treated this way! If this is what it's like to be treated like a king, I don't want anything of it! I wish everybody would treat me like I'm normal. Then maybe I could get out of here, I thought, staring angrily at my burger.

"Hi, Mart." Mom returned from the cafeteria with Dad to say goodnight. "The nurse told us you got sick on dinner. Aren't you feeling well tonight?"

In an act of vengeance, I jammed another fistful of french fries into my already stuffed mouth in anger. Tears poured down my cheeks, I choked, coughed up the food, then vomited whatever food had remained in my stomach. I pounded my fist on the table in rage.

"I can't take this anymore! I just want to go home! Why can't they just fix me and let me go home?"

Miss Linda rushed in with a roll of paper towel to replay a recent scene. Mom helped, assuring me everything would be okay. She always remained strong. I looked to my right at Dad, his arm set vertically on his leg and his forehead cupped in the palm of his hand. Flushed with despair, his eyes watered. He felt my pain but knew he could do no more than be at my side.

Flashbacks of my childhood accidents lit the movie screen in my memory. As an eight year old, I knelt down in our three-foot-deep swimming pool and sliced my knee open on a piece of glass beneath the liner. Blood dripped down my knee as I ran to Dad crying.

Dad couldn't stand the sight of blood, nor could he stand to see his children in pain, but there he sat next to me in the hospital after his son's near-death experience.

I reached over and placed my hand on his shoulder. "I'm going to be okay, Dad. I just want to go home and be with you and Mom and Cindy and Jeannette."

"I wish I could tell you when that day will be, Mart, but the doctors can't give us a day yet," he informed me.

I already knew that, but hearing it from my father was reason to worry. When I was a child, Dad was my god-figure because he always had the answers to all my questions. He could never be wrong because he was my Dad. He knew everything. But now he couldn't give me an answer to the most important question in my life. There was no light at the end of the tunnel. I felt like a Jew in a concentration camp, imprisoned without hope.

"Joan, would you come here a minute?" Miss Linda called from outside the room. "He's having a hard time keeping any food down. That was the second time he threw up. He's having a nervous reaction, so I'm going to give him something to calm him down."

"Do you have any idea what caused it?"

"I'm not sure, but I think it could be that he wants to leave, because he asked me earlier if I would take him out to the pie shop, and one of his friends asked me when Marty would be discharged because he said he really wanted to go home."

Mom and Dad left with a kiss and a promise to return next morning. At home that night, Mom and Dad found a poem, written by Jeannette, lying on her bed.

> To my dear brother Marty,
> > It must be a nightmare
> > I know it can't be true
> > I'm ready to wake up now
> > I've had enough
> > > Enough tears,
> > > Enough pain,
> > > Enough sorrow.
> > Yet each day when I awaken
> > I find myself still trapped—
> > Trapped in this ugly nightmare.
> > It must be a nightmare,
> > I know it can't be true,
> > Because God wouldn't punish
> > Someone like you.
> > > — Jeannette

I drifted off to sleep, yet remained awake in my dream. I saw myself leave my body, but also saw my body lying on the hospital bed. Like a ghost suspended in the air, I watched my body sleep on the bed. I was nervous. I twitched and turned in my sleep. I was restless.

"Why, God? Why did this have to happen to me?" I heard myself thinking in my sleep. "Please help me, Jesus. Just help me. I'll do anything if you just give me one more chance and save me. Don't leave me alone," I cried out.

As I hovered above the bed and watched myself sleep, a mysterious air seeped into the room, as if I were in a cemetery, closer to death. Or maybe I was watching myself dead. After all, what was I doing outside my own body? This isn't normal! This is the kind of news that only gets printed in tabloid papers. Is this an out-of-body experience like Shirley Maclaine has? If it is, it's disappointing, because she travels across the world when she departs. I'm still here in my own hospital room.

My body's energy diminished rapidly. I tried to remain suspended above the bed, but I felt myself falling back down into my own body on the bed. I awoke exhausted. My pillow, again, was soaked with tears.

All the crying and vomiting and conscious dreaming knocked me out, so when Mom and Dad arrived in the morning, I missed them because I had succumbed to a long period of peaceful sleep. Pure quietness, restful hours of slumber.

Maybe I'd be healed when I woke up, I thought, because God can do it for me.

He didn't this time.

When I awoke at dinnertime, Rob was by my side.

"How are you, Marty?"

As I looked up at him, relief beset me. I no longer felt the need to escape from the hospital because my best friend was by my side. He had been with me through some of the peak moments in my short-lived life, like when we got our first jobs together at a restaurant. Like when we played doubles on the tennis team at high school. We were Big Rob and the Bruiser, managers of the varsity basketball team last year when the Cougars advanced to the Sweet 16. We even produced the infamous BigRoBruiser candy bar. We shopped for girls at the mall. And we led our church softball team through victorious seasons and brought home championship trophies two consecutive years.

We were even together during the sad times, like when my light blue parakeet, Perry, died and we built a wooden coffin for him, then dug a hole out back and buried him.

"I'm okay, Rob, but I want to get out of here. Can you help me?"

Rob looked at me with an I'm-helpless-but-I-want-to-help look in his eyes. He'd come to the hospital each and every day but three.

My time at the hospital tinged my memory with cloudy pictures of people coming and going in my room. Memories were vague. Everybody came to see me, though, I remember. Friends of Mom and Dad, friends of mine. It seemed everybody who knew me came to visit, as if to pay their last respects at my funeral.

Chapter 5

"**M**om, Rob's Mom is here with the station-wagon to take Marty," Jeannette reported. "Does she know we're taking him to the rehabilitation center across from Alexian Brothers Medical Center?"

"Yes, I told her. Just go downstairs with Dad, Cindy and Rob and wait for us," she said.

Nurses wheeled a stretcher into the room and transferred me from the bed. I pleaded with God under my breath that I could go home and rest in my own bed. But I knew that wouldn't happen. My body would be delivered to another layer of hell. Would they again pierce my body like a voodoo doll and jam needles into my arm, wrap bandages around my leg and connect my body with liquid-filled tubes and leave me helpless?

From a hospital to a rehab center. Like a Jew in slavery led from one desert to another. Moses and the Red Sea were nowhere in sight. How long will it be, oh Lord?

I realized there was no running away from my condition. Wherever I was, there I would be, broken. And I'd need more than Moses to get me across the Red Sea. I'd need a lot of hands to carry me.

A half-hour later, they wheeled me into a new room. Niehoff Pavilion, my new home. Friends and family stayed all day. Some through the night. Offering help. Asking me what I wanted. If I needed anything. They stood over me. With hurt in their eyes. Time and time again they replayed their mourner's role. Couldn't they see how much it was hurting me to see them grieve? I needed their smiles and friendship.

The pain was excruciating. My soul was enduring eternal punishment. Alone in my own deep, dark cold cellar. Blind to hope. Lost, where no angels of mercy could ever find me. Down a long trail of lifeless night where other souls fell by the wayside, shattered and broken. I searched ahead for a light of hope and cried out, "My God, please help me! Just give me one more chance! Save me from this hell!"

The days passed slowly and I awoke each morning with my pillow soaked from tears, again, safe in my own purgatory, but unable to walk, think or even speak like I used to. I'd repeat the same sentences to visitors because my short-term memory had all but burnt out.

"Marianne! Surprised to see you. Thanks for coming," I told a high school friend. "I'm so surprised you're here. Thanks a lot for coming to see me." Even those with whom I hadn't developed intimate friendships, those I knew no more than in passing in the school hallways or sat with in classrooms came to visit me.

Excited about my surprise visitor, I thanked her again for coming, told her once again how surprised I was, and then attempted my first daring act since the accident.

"Marianne, watch me. I think I can walk on a walker," I told her, swinging my fully-casted leg across the bed to the right side. I lifted my left arm with my right, then reached over for the walker. "I haven't tried this yet, so this is my first time."

She stood across the room and watched me struggle to gain my balance. With both feet on the ground and two hands on the walker, I felt like a tightrope walker on a high wire above Niagara Falls. Concentrating intensely on each step, my heart pounded faster. I moved my right foot, then leaned forward on the walker and slid my left foot up even with the right. Another step with the right, pressure on the walker, slid the left foot even with the right. I took five steps around the front of the bed, leaned forward on the walker when, "Aaaagggggghhhh!" I lost my balance and fell to my right, banged my head on the wall and landed on the floor hurt.

Marianne froze with fear. A girl much smaller than I was, she could do nothing. A nun walked past the room and glanced in.

"Oh, my! Are you all right? Stay there and let me get some help."

Days and nights became a fierce struggle to even want to live. Sessions with a speech therapist to help me regain my memory and improve word comprehension were a rerun of elementary school days.

He sat behind a large oak desk and read parts of a short story. Then, he fired across vocabulary questions at me. I drew blanks. Couldn't remember. Didn't know. Made no sense to me.

"Let's try comprehension," he said. "What did Fred mean when he said, 'Disobedience would be self-defeating.'?"

"Tony told Fred—no, wait a minute. That's right. Fred said that. Not Tony." I paused. Thought a moment. Forgot the question. "Could you repeat the question? I'm sorry. I don't remember what you asked."

My brain was a platter of scrambled eggs. Head therapy seemed futile. I felt part of my mind working. It strained to recall word definitions. I knew them once. I'd used those words my whole life. Understanding what the therapist had read was difficult too. I thought it would help if he let me read the stories with my own eyes. I was more visual than auditory. I began reading on my own at night hoping it would help my concentration and memory.

I was determined not to let my impairment hinder my development, whether physical, intellectual, or emotional.

In physical therapy on my back, I summoned all the energy in my body to raise my left arm. My arm felt like a ton of steel. I remembered how easily I had tossed a tennis ball up into the air. Gently. Lightly. C'mon, Marty, the same way as before. Try to imagine it's all in your head and that you can lift your am. Progress, by my standards, was sub-minimal. "Never be satisfied until you know you're at your peak," I remember hearing in my head when I ran. So I pushed harder and harder and harder until I'd strained so hard my face turned beet red. My arm moved inches at first. I continued to force it higher and higher through the weeks.

> To Marty:
>> He's getting better
>> I know he's getting better
>> Each day I see him,
>> I notice some improvement.
>> But how long?
>> How long will he be like this?
>> How long will the pain and suffering go on?
>> The worst is over.
>> The nightmare is gone, I hope.
>> But the memory of this tragic ordeal
>> Will last forever.
>> Forever!
>> The word has a meaning I cannot explain.
>> It's too long.
>> Too long to leave such a terrible memory
>> like this in one's mind.
>>> — Jeannette

Day in and day out I yelled to God. "Come on, Lord! I'm doing my part. Why don't You give me a little bit more help? This isn't easy, You know." I felt like quitting at times, yet something sustained me. I could feel it. Intangible, but present and real enough for me.

Dad lifted my hopes and helped me to see the finish line. "I drew up this calendar. Here's today's date, and if you look down here, that's the day we're going to bring you home. And I've got a special breakfast planned for that morning, and later on in the afternoon, we're going to watch the Fighting Irish play Michigan in the college football game of the week."

Grandpa and Grandma Folan were from Ireland. Dad was proud to be Irish and brought his children up proud to be Folans. I became a big Fighting Irish fan growing up, everybody knew it, even Fr. Greg, who brought me a genuine Notre Dame football helmet.

Touched by his love for humanity, and me in particular, I thanked him. Always able to look at life a little less seriously than most people, he joked with me. "I just wish I had given it to you before you went out on the bike ride. That way, you could've ridden with the helmet on."

I gained greater dexterity of my hands and fingers a few weeks later. I felt farther along in recovery, almost near a state of happiness. By starting over with simple exercises, whether with my mind, leg, or fingers, and slowly making progress, I felt a sense of achievement. Nurses wheeled me into the cafeteria twice a week in the evenings for a ceramics class.

"Dad, look what I'm making for you," I said, showing him a golf bag pencil holder I was painting green with black trim. "And I'm going to make Jeannette a cupcake to put her jewelry in. If you hold the cherry on top and take off the lid, she can put her things inside."

Ceramics class helped me feel as though I had accomplished something for the first time since the accident.

As I laid back at night and prayed to God, I recalled some of the Bible stories I'd learned in catechism on Saturday mornings. The desert scenes especially. I remember Jesus spent 40 days and nights in the desert with no food. There was nobody out there with him either. Except Satan. He couldn't have been very good company. Jesus must have been lonely. I wonder if this was how he felt. Maybe. But I'll bet he grew even weaker than me because he didn't have any food. At least I had Miss Nice Nurse Linda to serve me practically anything I wanted, even pumpkin pie.

I'm sorry if I'm thinking only about myself, Lord. But I'm a mess.

Emotionally, I vacillated between heaven and hell.

Today, I saw him walk
I couldn't believe it.
I just wanted to cry
When I saw how much he was struggling
How each small step, took his complete
concentration and strength,
I wanted to scream
It's not fair.
It's not fair for such a wonderful person
so active in his sports and with his friends,
Be hurt for no reason at all.
It's just not fair.
                              — Jeannette

I left the rehab center Thursday, September 17, after sixty-nine days. I felt as if I had been born again, fresh and new. I felt as if I could walk on water, like Jesus. For the first time since the accident, I could raise my left hand as high as my head! I could really do it! Not only was I free to go home, but I felt myself healing. Maybe my recovery was only a few weeks around the corner. After all, I rationalized, Jesus rose on the third day.

Rob's Mom accompanied Mom to Niehoff Pavilion to pick me up. They celebrated my departure by taking me out to lunch. They too shared in my happiness and ate with me.

Food. When we win in sports, we celebrate by going out to eat. "Pizza for everybody," coaches yell out loud. We lose, we pat each other on the back and say, "That's okay. Let's go get something to eat and forget about it." No in-betweens. Food is always the answer.

I smelled the aroma of hot Italian lasagna wafting above me. My mouth watered, my eyes searched for the prize meal. No more hospital food! A true victory in itself, I declared myself a free prisoner returning to life as I knew it. Life at home meant Mom's home-cooked meals. And Dad's special breakfasts in the morning with Irish songs playing on the radio. I couldn't wait to hear Dad yell out after fixing one of his cheese soufflés, or brown scrambled egg meals, "Come and git it 'fore I fling it to the hogs!" Oh, those cheerful Saturday mornings. Back in my own bed with my own pillow. I couldn't wait to pet Genie and Heidi again, our two German shepherds. And Tiffany, the little short-haired terrier. To me she was an oversized rodent.

Life was getting back to the way it always was. For the next several months, I struggled between living in the past and accepting myself in the here-and-now.

◆　　◆　　◆

"Mom, can we stop by school to see the volleyball team?" I asked, wanting to see my friends whom I had reported on the past three years for the weekly high school newspaper. I wanted badly to return to school to cover girls sports for the *Conant Crier*, a paper recognized as one of the best high school newspapers in the nation.

Volleyball, basketball, and softball teams listed, for the most part, the same players on their rosters: Kathy Williams, Deanna Lacko, Brenda Schumacher and others, all of whom had visited me the past months.

Mom didn't object to stopping by, so after lunch we drove to Conant.

As I walked down the hallway with my walker, I felt welcomed by the walls, even the sniff of air smelled homey. I sighed with relief each step I took closer to the gymnasium. I could hear the sounds of gym shoes squeaking on the floor. Bodies diving to save shots. Volleyballs slapping against bare arms.

"Betsy! Dawnell! Hi, everybody!" I said, hobbling into the gym where they were playing against arch-rival Schaumburg.

After the match, they welcomed me back and presented me with cards and a team picture, an expression of their care.

"I can't tell you how much this means to me," I said, lost for words, yet deeply touched by their thoughtfulness.

"So when will you be back in school to report on us?" Debbie Lewis asked. "I don't think anybody else is going to do it besides you, so they need you on the *Crier* staff."

"I'll be home this semester with a tutor, but I'll be back before the year ends to do some reporting. I'll still come and see your volleyball games even though I won't be reporting on them. I have to spend time on my studies."

I felt like a soldier returning home from war. Crippled. Almost helpless. Yet loved.

Dear Marty,

Welcome home! You've been through a lot these past two months, seven days. We all have. Every night I cried for you. Every night. I know you must have cried too. But although you've made it home, finally, you still have more to come. All I want to say is that I know you still hurt and still need someone to talk to. We may not have been very close, but if you ever need me, I want you to know, I care, I love you and I want to help you. You mean a lot to me and Mom, Dad and Cindy and all your friends. All of us love you and want to help.

Every night I said a prayer for you, but soon I realized it wasn't worth it. Not that I didn't care what happened to you; but I didn't think

God was listening. 'Cause if He was, He would have heard me when I prayed the day before the accident: "That Marty, Mom, Dad, Cindy and all of my friends, neighbors, and relatives would live another healthy, happy day."

I prayed that He would watch over us while we were apart. And that soon we would be together again.

Many times when I couldn't fall asleep, like tonight, I'd write poems or notes, like this one. Maybe someday, when the hurting stops and the accident is not always on your mind, I'll show them to you.

Dear Marty,

I reread this note and decided it be best if I didn't give it to you. Not now. But I don't know how I'm going to tell you how much I care. How much I love you and want to help. I'm sure I'll find some way. I hope I do the right thing. What's best for you is that you get well. And once again be my brother, Marty. The "Bruiser" to your friends. Mom and Dad's son, and everyone's favorite guy.

I don't know why this happened to you. Out of all the dirty, low-down, sneaky punks in this world, why did this have to happen to you, Marty?

With love,
Jeannette

Chapter 6

October 17, I was freed from the cast. As I lay down on my right side on the doctor's table, he slid his razor blade-like tool from the top of the cast on my hip all the way down to my foot, then removed it. Freed from the plastic encasement, I felt the cool air caress my legs.

"Now, I want you to lift your leg as high as you can," he said.

Emotion built up inside me as I prepared to make every effort to lift my leg. Somehow, I knew it wasn't going to be easy. I thought back to the race I had run the weekend before my accident when all the energy inside me propelled my body forward with astounding strength and remarkable speed I'd never achieved before. I remembered the adrenaline rush before the gun went off. I remembered the tension in the air.

Now on the doctor's table, I silently prayed that the same power flow through me once again.

"Okay, here it goes," I told the doctor and my family audience. "Ugggggghhhhh!"

I struggled to lift the family of elephants on my leg. I couldn't lift it even a fraction of an inch. But determination empowered me as I tried again.

"Uuuuuuuggggggghhhhhhh! It's not budging an inch, doctor," I said, not daring to admit defeat, but waiting for the secret from the doctor on how to lift it. I was certain that after giving it so much time to heal that I should be able to lift it. Maybe I was doing something wrong, or maybe he really had my leg tied down to the table and he was playing a trick on me.

"Your gluteus medius in your left hip is weak," he said. "Those are the exercises you need to do at home. Lie down on your right side and try to lift your leg. It'll move eventually, but you'll need to do the exercises daily."

He wasn't joking. Those elephants were real. I found no consolation in the message framed on the wall. "The sufferings of the present time are not worthy to be compared to the glory which shall be revealed in us (Romans 8:18)."

Morning, noon, and night, every day, every week, every month. Exercise and prayer became a one-in-the-same religion, and God, my only helper. I continued to beg for His help, and I begged those elephants to go on a diet.

"Just help me lift it up one inch this week...please!"

Weekly evaluations. "Dad, come and measure how high I can lift it!" I'd call out from the hallway, as I lay on the carpet with my back up against the wall. One inch was the first of many milestones to come. I felt like a baby learning how to walk. Step by step. Inch by inch.

Looking back from the dreadful days at Sherman Hospital, I realized how far I had come. A psychologist once said that those who have the healthiest psyches are the ones who can live off past experiences yet also project into the future in a balanced way. The past I had no problem with. It was all rainbows and rose gardens. The present and future were more like rainstorms and thorns.

I devoted my days to exercise and studying at home. The school year had begun, yet I missed out on the first semester of my senior year, what was supposed to be the best year of life for a high school student. A tutor spent hours with me each week on math and English. My favorite subject since first grade, math became my crisis course due to the brain damage. "Identify the numerical values of sine and co-sine," she'd say, leading me through trigonometry.

"I think it's..." I struggled to remember the numbers she had read to me only moments before. I was an A student in mathematics from elementary school up through junior year, but now the math wires in my brain were short-circuited, my short-term memory still unable to recall information. "...I don't know! I can't remember!" I choked on my own words, trying to fight my inability to remember. I felt my brain trying to perform the functions, but it couldn't. I felt frustrated.

Jeannette, Cindy, Mom and Dad felt sorry for me, but my pain was theirs too, each in their own way.

I've cried more tears than have ever been shed
I've prayed more prayers than have ever been said.
I've hoped and I've wished
For the best to come true
And that God would help to guide you through
Through the tears, the pain, and the scars left behind
I searched for an answer I just couldn't find.
I asked and I prayed to the Lord up above,
Why did this happen?
Could it be out of love?

I'm still so confused,
I just don't understand
So I ask and I pray for God's helping hand
As the days and the weeks slowly pass by
I keep asking over and over—why?
                    — Jeannette

I prayed every morning when I awoke. Every moment I exercised on the carpet in the hallway, I prayed. The last one I'd talk to at night before bed was my God. I'd made progress, a considerable amount, in my ability to walk. My leg shot up five inches high! I exercised determinedly. Still in a fierce struggle to return to my pre-accident condition, I was bound and committed for all my life was worth. That was the only reason worth living.

Then one night, I sat alone on a couch in the family room. The only light was a candle on the table to my right. I reflected on my life and sank into a quicksand of depression.

I could slam-dunk a basketball. I ran the fastest race of my life. And I'm sure I would've run faster if I'd kept running and training. I was intelligent and earned above-average grades. I could play tennis. I could work. I could go out with girls. My life was fun! I don't know if I'll ever be able to do any of that ever again! I don't want to suffer like this anymore. I want to do everything I used to be able to do! I can't stand this! I felt my heart beating faster, as my face turned red and I began to sweat. My mind had raced me forward, faster, faster, and even faster, right up to the edge of life's cliff. I slammed on the brakes, caught my breath and teetered on the edge, hanging over. My thoughts now: *Life has no purpose. If I can't do what I used to be able to do, life isn't worth living anymore. I'll end it. I'll end the pain and suffering, for myself and for everyone who doesn't like to see my hurting like this. I'll commit suicide.*

Throughout the next three weeks, I devised several plans to kill myself.

I'll shoot myself in the head, that way it'll end instantly and I won't suffer. It'll be like blinking, and I'll end it. Maybe taking drugs and overdosing would be a more peaceful and less messy way of doing it. I could pump my body full of drugs before I go to sleep, and that way I could die in my sleep. I'd never wake up. Or I could end it all the way it should've happened. I'll jump in front of a vehicle and kill myself.

I dwelled on the thought of suicide and wondered how it would affect my family, friends, neighbors and everyone else who had helped me so far. They wouldn't have to see me suffer anymore because I'd be gone.

Each morning when I woke up, every afternoon, and the last thing before bed, like a machine programmed to perform certain functions, I'd drop my body on the carpet in the hallway, lay back against the wall and lift my leg up and down, up and down, repetition after repetition. Constant prayer I'd breathe with every repetition.

"Jesus Lord, have mercy on me. Help me through my suffering."

Apart from exercise, I didn't beg for help. I knew my life would end. I didn't want to live.

Marty was talking on the phone to Marianne
I don't know whether he wants sympathy or what
He said he can't stop looking at the bad side of
things
Ever since his accident, he can't understand why
everything has gone wrong.
Then he said something that made me cry.
He said, "Maybe I would just be better off dead.
"Why didn't I just die?"
I just stood there. I couldn't stop crying.
I don't understand any of this either.
But I want Marty to get better. Please take the bad
thoughts away from Marty. Please!
I love him so much! Please! Help me so I can help
him.
I love him so much!
— Jeannette

Late in January, I prepared to say goodbye.

"Fr. Greg," I quietly whispered to the one man I trusted like a guardian angel, "I've thought about it for the past month. You know what I've been through. You know the condition I used to be in. Remember the day Rob and I beat you and your brother Adrian in basketball? Remember how I could slam-dunk the ball?

"Well, I'll never be able to do that ever again. Look at the condition I'm in. I'm practically a vegetable. Life is no fun anymore. Christmas came and went, and it was like I didn't even know it. Life means nothing to me, so I've decided to end it."

"End it? I'm not sure what you mean, Marty," he said, gazing at me quizzically.

"I mean I'm going to commit suicide. You're the only one I'm telling before I do it, though, because you're the one I've been able to tell all my secrets to. But I realize things just aren't going to be the way they used to be."

"Marty, I can't say that I know what you are going through, because I'm sure nobody can even try to imagine all the physical and emotional pain you are suffering. You're right when you say you could once slam-dunk a basketball. You were an excellent athlete. Not just in basketball, but in all sports. You were in very good condition. In fact, I would say that the reason you didn't lose your leg in the accident was because you kept it in such good condition."

"Yeah, that's what the doctor says."

"So you see, it's not just me who is saying that. The doctors even told you, and they are experts in what they do, so you know I'm not just telling you because I'm your friend. What I'm telling you, Marty, is you didn't die for a reason. You aren't happy with the way things are now, but look at yourself by how you've come back in just the past six months," he spoke in amazement. "You were in a coma, not able to even move. You've gone from a wheelchair to a walker to crutches, and now you're using a cane. You couldn't even move your arm, and now you can move it about freely. And I remember you couldn't even go to school last semester. And this semester you're going every other day. Marty, as I look at all the progress you've made, I say that's tremendous! I think if you keep it up, no doubt you'll be up and running and playing basketball again sooner than you think."

I trust him. He's right. Maybe someday I'll play basketball again. Maybe I will run again.

No, no, no. Not maybe. I will! I know someday I will do it, I convinced myself, tears flooding my eyes as I wrestled with the enemy of confidence—doubt.

Sunday at church, Fr. Greg handed me a card with a poem written on it. I read the words of encouragement, learned them, memorized them, embodied them and prayed over them every breathing moment of the day.

DON'T QUIT

When things go wrong, as they sometimes will
When the road you're trudging seems all uphill
When funds are low and debts are high
And you want to smile, but have to sigh
When care is pressing you down a bit
Rest if you must, but don't quit.

Life is strange with its twists and turns
As every one of us sometimes learns
And many a fellow turns about
When he might have won had he stuck it out
Don't give up though the pace seems slow
You may succeed with another blow.

Often the goal is nearer than
It seems to a fair and faltering man
Often the struggler has given up
When he might have captured the victor's cup
And he learned too late when night came down
How close he was to the golden crown.

Success is failure turned inside out
The silver tint of the clouds of doubt
And you never can tell how close you are
It may be near when it seems afar
So stick to the fight when you're hardest hit
It's when things seem worst, that you mustn't quit.

Chapter 7

I fell asleep quickly that night, then into a deep dream state where I saw all my friends and family members. There were hundreds of them. Hot dogs and hamburgers smoked up the barbecue grill. Chips, potato salad, ice cream, pop, beer, and lemonade were served as they gathered together on picnic blankets. The mood was festive. Everyone was jubilant. Boys and girls threw water balloons at one other. Music played, people danced and still another group at the west end of the park bumped, set, and spiked a volleyball in the sand. I could hear Mom and Dad remark about how happy they were that Jeannette had found a nice man to marry and that Cindy was finally pregnant with her first.

My old friend Mike reclined in a sand chair next to some guy named Jim. They drank from cold bottles of beer. I watched myself, as if on a movie screen, yet I could feel the sun's heat on my face and bare arms. A mild wind blew warm air upon my face. As Mike drank, I could taste the flavor of his beer and I liked it. I'd never tasted beer before. And how could I taste it if he was drinking it? School chums stuffed their faces with hot dogs and stood around the grill and talked with my relatives about me. I watched them bite the dogs and, somehow, tasted what they ate. "Not enough onion and too much mustard," I told them.

"Hey, Karen," I waved to a friend from high school. My favorite volleyball player and a darn good badminton player, too, Karen Drahos stood next to a tall man with a baby in her arms. They were laughing, so they couldn't hear me.

"Marty always gave a hundred percent, especially when he trained for those long races," she told one of our classmates. "That spilled over into everything he did. From sports to studies and from helping people to...well, I was going to say helping himself, but I guess I can't say that anymore."

Her voice faded. I couldn't understand what she had said. What did she mean, "I guess I can't say that anymore," in regard to helping myself. I darn near drove myself into the ground physically and mentally overcoming that accident. I'd probably worked just as hard in rehabilitation as some athletes do in training for the Olympics. I put a lot into everything I did, so don't tell me I didn't. I want to be remembered as someone who gave more than one hundred percent. I want them to remember me as not being a quitter. I busted my butt seven days a week training for the 10-km road run and I ran the fastest race of my life. My imagination couldn't have run that fast. If I hadn't crashed my bike, I probably could have continued training and won the race next year. Maybe even run in the state cross-country finals. Who knows, maybe I could have begun training for the Olympics, and made the team, and won the gold! "To be remembered..." the words lingered in my mind. This get-together was just that: a memorial gathering.

The mood turned dismal as a small group of classmates formed a circle and silence befell them. Rob, Mike, Jim, Scott, and Kristy set their lunch plates on the ground and joined hands. "Lord, we thank You for this food and for all the people who have joined together this day once again to remember Marty. We know he rests beside You in heaven, yet we still grieve his parting from this earth after so many years. We miss him still. As we continue to meet each year to remember not only his passing on, but more importantly his life and the positive influence he had on each of us, we too become more aware of the inevitability of death and of our own mortality. Help us to live each day more fully and completely, Lord. We offer this prayer through Christ our Lord, Amen." As Rob finished praying, each of them took a tissue and wiped the tears from their eyes.

What the heck is going on? I'm right here! Don't waste your time remembering who I was or what I did. I'm alive, here and now! I frantically yelled to the crowd, but no one acknowledged my presence. I reached out to touch them on the arms and hands, but my ghost-like hand couldn't make contact with them. I was invisible, a spirit who had returned from the after-life. Was this my purgatory? Would I now until forever lead a life on earth among my close friends and relatives without being able to communicate with them?

I don't want to be a memory! Please, Lord. I'll try harder next time! Just give me one more chance! I'll make something out of my life.

Chapter 8

So many people say he's getting better.
So many people say he'll be okay.
But I'm not sure.
One day he acts the way he used to.
The next day, he seems slow, confused.
Sometimes I laugh or joke about the accident.
But deep down inside, I'm always crying
I feel empty now —
As if someone had taken out my insides and
left nothing;
Just an awful feeling of fear, confusion and
loneliness.
I know many times we would fight,
And I know he sometimes didn't like me or my
friends,
But when something like this happens,

It makes you look at things differently.
I love him. I want him to get better soon.
Please, Marty. Please get better.
                              — Jeannette

"**D**ad, I can get my leg all the way up!" I shouted to him from the hallway. Immediately he ran over to see my accomplishment and congratulate me. "Now do you think I can go out and try to run?" I asked, feeling supremely confident.

He looked at me, not wanting to tell me the truth, because he knew it would hurt my feelings. He wanted to see me run, but he knew it wasn't time yet.

"Let's first make sure that it's okay to run because you still have a pin in your leg, so we have to see what the doctor says about going out and running," he said, still leaving me room for hope.

A month passed, progress was gradual, but never good enough to suit me, so I exercised repetitions of twenty-five, three sets, then four, then five. Three times a day wasn't enough, so five became my routine.

Closer to my first day running, hope and anticipation built up inside me.

Days later. "Doctor, do you think it's safe for me to go out and run?" I asked, having made a return visit to Sherman Hospital for x-rays.

"Hmmmm..." he said examining the x-rays in front of a fluorescent light in his office. "You can keep the pin in your leg however long you want. In fact, you could keep it in there for the rest of your life if you want to, but it seems to me by the x-rays here that you have some calcium deposits in this area here, and that seems to be hindering proper growth of the bone. My suggestion is that we take it out."

"Yes! Take it out! That's great!" I rejoiced, not giving any thought to being sliced open on an operating table again.

Mom, however, couldn't bear the thought of seeing me cut up again. She broke down in tears.

"Mom, it's okay. I want it done. I'd rather get it over with so this doesn't bother me anymore and I can run again," I said, putting my arm around her shoulder.

Inches of progress were adding up to miles of confidence, self-assurance and, more than anything else, hope.

Back home later that afternoon, I heralded the great news to Dad, hoping he would share in the joyful surprise.

"Dad, the doctor said I can have the pin taken out! He said it's okay to run now if you go along with me."

The following weekend marked a seven-month anniversary from my personal best 10-km run.

"Are you ready, Dad?" I asked him as I tied my running shoes. Still with a heavy limp, I carried my cane with me for support.

"All ready, let's go!" Dad cheered me on as we walked out the front door on a mild February afternoon.

My stride wasn't the same. I wasn't lifting my leg as high or stretching it out as far. I seemed to expect a miracle that when I went out to run, everything would return to how it used to be. Frustrated, yet determined, I pushed on, dragging my left leg behind me, jamming the rubber-tipped cane down on the sidewalk ahead of me to help me maintain my balance.

Damnit! This isn't the way I want to run. I cursed myself under my breath, feeling the heavy metal rod up near my hipbone. Just wait until I get this pin taken out, then everything will change. I talked myself into believing a miracle would happen when I wanted.

"How does the leg feel, Mart?" Dad asked, gasping for air.

"It's not the way I thought it was going to be, Dad. It's dragging, and I can feel the pin in my hip. It doesn't hurt, but I can feel something there."

"Well, you have to be patient with it, Mart. That leg hasn't had much time to become strong and heal the way you want it to so you can run again," he said.

One week later I returned to Sherman Hospital for the operation. In and out in a matter of hours, the pin was removed. What I imagined to be a two-inch thin piece of metal came out as part of the Alaskan pipeline. It was an 18-inch long rod.

Free at last!

I continued to walk with the cane because I still limped. The gluteus medius was still weak. It wasn't the pin that had caused the limp.

My exercises continued five times a day, pushing, pushing, and pushing harder, wanting to see progress day by day. Angry that I didn't.

"Honey, why don't you let up on that for awhile? Don't hurt yourself," Mom said, still hurt emotionally from nearly losing her only son.

"Mom, I've got to. The leg isn't going to get any better by itself," I said, feeling isolated from the rest of the world, even my family.

I am alone in my own world. Nobody knows what it's like in here...this hell. God, why can't You just send down an angel to perform a miracle for me to make me better? There is no meaning to any of this! God, I'm making everybody's life miserable, including my own.

As I continued exercising, I noticed blood dripping out onto the newly laid plush carpet from where my hip was stitched. I felt helpless, yet responsible for staining the carpet.

"Damnit!" I cried in anguish. "Mom! Come here a minute!" I yelled out, breaking down in tears because of the guilt I felt.

"Oh, honey, don't worry about it. I'll clean it up," she said, hiding her own feelings over the incident. "Did your stitches pop open?"

"No, they're still together. Just leaking. I'm sorry, Mom. If I knew it was dripping out, I would've gotten up. I'll watch it closer next time. I promise."

The off-brown, lightly tanned carpet had rubbed a trademark rash on the side of my right leg, signifying the grueling work I demanded from myself.

The dried, six-inch round brown-red stain on the carpet marked my territory, my battlefield where I'd spilled my blood.

Chapter 9

A nother painful blow to the family, as a result of my accident, came when the administrators at James B. Conant High School called Mom and Dad in for a conference and suggested I drop a few classes, and wait until summer school to graduate.

"Yes, I understand your reasons for suggesting he drop a few courses and make the load a bit lighter on himself," Dad told Dr. Manos, the principal. "But before I tell you to go ahead and take him out of his classes and schedule him for summer school, I'd like for his Mom and me to return home and talk with him about it. I think he should be the one to make the decision."

Psychology was a fascinating subject for me second semester in Ms. Oldberg's class.

"Mom, Dad, look what it says here in the textbook about head traumas and memory loss," I told them as they walked into the house.

"Mart, your Mom and I would like to talk with you a minute," Dad said, sitting down at the kitchen table with me. "We had a talk with the administrative staff at Conant, and they think it would be better for you to drop a few classes and graduate in the summer. That way you could take your time and not have to work as hard on so many classes."

Caught off guard. I didn't expect to hear what they were telling me. How could they want to do this to me? Like Fr. Greg said, I've come so far since my accident. Don't they realize that? And how about all my friends I grew up with? I want to graduate with them!

Another mountain stood in front of me. This one, I didn't want to climb.

"What did you tell them, Dad?"

"I told them that it wasn't for your mother and me to decide for you, but that we would go home and talk with you about it," he said, softening the blow.

Still frantic, in a state of panic, I stood my own ground, knowing my prayer was already being answered as I spoke to them. "Mom, Dad, I just want a chance. I don't want to drop any classes, because I'm doing the best job I can in all of them now and I think that if I keep it up, I could graduate on time, instead of in the summer. I know I'm not doing very well in trigonometry, but I think if I spent extra time studying my homework and going to the math tutor at school, I could do better and pass the class. So I really don't want to drop any classes. I just want a chance, that's all."

I felt compelled to drive out every possible demon of reason for the class-drop/summer-graduation plan with a new plan of my own.

Mom and Dad seemed ambivalent. They knew my dropping a few courses would allow me extra time to study more diligently the few classes I needed to study for. They didn't want to see me miserable, forcing myself to make the grade in all my classes when it would be easier to comply with the administrators' plan.

"I'll call them tomorrow from work and tell them," Dad said, supporting my decision.

"Dad, remember when we used to watch the Notre Dame games and you'd tell me they'd always say, 'Win one for the Gipper'?"

"Yes," Dad nodded, unaware of where I was leading him.

"Well, I'm going to win, too!" I promised, before I burst into tears and went to my bedroom, fearful of the challenge ahead of me, yet determined. The administrative staff dared me to accept the challenge to climb their mountain, all the way to the top.

Fueled with anger, yet motivated to prove myself, I attended school five days a week beginning in March. Still unable to maintain my balance well enough to carry my books and folders up and down stairs, I asked a classmate to leave class with me five minutes before the end of each period. By the time school would end and I'd get into Mom's car and make it home, all I had energy for was to fall on my bed and sleep.

God, where are You now? How am I supposed to last through every day like this up to the end of the school year? I haven't even started my homework assignments that are due for tomorrow. I told them I just wanted a chance, but God, I don't know how I'm going to do it, I cried silently.

Barely able to move, I dragged myself off the bed, plopped down on the carpet in the hall and lifted my leg, up and down.

"Ugh, push, push, push!" I yelled to the leg, seeming separated from the rest of my body. "Don't quit. You can do it. You're going to run again, you sonofabitch! Ohhh..." The leg dropped, exhausting the rest of my body.

Physically, I was spent. Emotionally, wrecked. But no matter how I felt, my body carried itself to the hall, threw me down on the carpet and demanded me to summon all the strength I could muster to improve my dilapidated condition.

My entire focus of life was on me and me only. I didn't care if the Chicago Bears, Bulls or Blackhawks won or lost, like I used to. I didn't watch the games or even read the stories in the newspapers. I seldom watched television. I didn't listen to the radio. Drawn into myself, I needed to find the one tiny corner in my heart where peace resided. That corner was my past.

"Dr. Nelson, I'm going to school every day of the week, just like I did before my accident," I told the school psychologist eight weeks into the second semester, "but I can't play basketball. I'm going to miss it. I remember I could slam-dunk a ball before the accident. Rob and I played on a church league team and we were real good. We were also managers of the varsity team here our sophomore year when they almost went downstate to the championship. That's when we got the nicknames 'Big Rob' and 'Bruiser.'"

For the next ten minutes I recalled the past few years of my life when I had direction. When I led a life of accomplishment. When life had purpose.

"Marty, that was in the past," Dr. Nelson confronted me. "You're not there anymore."

"But is my life always going to be like this? If it is, then I don't want...it to be," I caught myself before blurting out that I wanted to end it. I hadn't thought of suicide since I last spoke with Fr. Greg, when the plan slowly vanished from my mind, as my anger and ambition drove me through rehabilitation in a hurried fury in which I had no time to think about driving myself to the grave.

"Marty, you need to find yourself." Dr. Nelson's last words were burned into my brain.

I wandered through the days and weeks pondering his declarative statement.

Find myself? What does he mean? I'm right here. I've found myself. I'm miserable because I was almost killed and I'm unable to do anything I used to be able to do. I'll probably never be able to do anything again anyway. That's the way it is. So there, Dr. Nelson, I've found myself.

Nods and smiles from classmates as I walked in the halls. Even the big macho three-sport athletes set aside their self-righteous attitudes and congratulated me for progress made thus far. Couldn't they see my fear, behind my facade of determination and effort? Was I fooling them, or was I really fooling myself?

"Spring was born today," I scribbled in my journal. "I can jog, slow, but the limp is noticeable. I can't play tennis because I can't move around the court fast enough to get to the ball. I feel miserable. Like I'm broken apart in a million pieces on the inside. I have to spend most of my time studying if I want to graduate on time with the class. I wonder what I'd be like if I hadn't gone out riding that day? I probably would have kept running and maybe I would have won a race. Maybe I could have been a super cross-country runner and won awards. At least my legs would be in better condition than they are now. I sure would be doing a lot better in math, too. Rob has not been a good friend since I got home from the hospital. I can't understand why."

◆　　◆　　◆

"Dr. Nelson, he was my friend," I told him the next week in therapy. "We were best friends, like brothers, almost. We were Big Rob and the Bruiser. We got our first jobs together as dishwashers at a restaurant. We played tennis together as a doubles team. Picked up girls at shopping centers together. Managed the varsity team and even played basketball together. We were co-captains of a championship softball team together. Now he doesn't even return my phone calls or come over anymore. I don't understand it."

"You're saying things aren't the same as they were before the accident," he said.

I heard this story before. Everything changes, he's telling me. Stop living in the past, Marty. Accept the here-and-now.

"I know what you're saying. But what I'm saying is I don't understand why it is that I'm the one who was almost killed and he's the one who leaves his best friend."

"You say he was your best friend and you did all these things together, until the accident happened, then he left you?"

"Well, not exactly. Mom made a list of everybody who came to Sherman Hospital and Rob came all but three days. But I just don't understand how he could leave me after all we'd been through," I explained, trying to make sense of a once-golden friendship. "We were even supposed to go bike riding that day, but he had to cut the lawn, so he said he'd meet me at the softball game at church."

"Did you say he was supposed to go on the bike ride with you that day?"

"Yes, we always went on bike rides. In fact, the day before the accident, we rode ten miles, then came home to play tennis like we always did."

"Marty, you say Rob and you were very close, almost like brothers, and that you used to go out on bike rides together. And the day of your accident was the one time Rob couldn't go with you. And now he doesn't talk to you or come over like he used to. What does that tell you?"

"I don't know," I said, thinking it was Dr. Nelson's job to figure it all out, not mine.

"What that tells me is that maybe he feels guilty for your accident. Maybe he thinks that if he had gone with you on that bike ride, as he always had, you wouldn't have gotten hit."

Like a missing puzzle piece that was found and fit, the entire picture came into focus.

"You've begun recovering, but maybe he never will. You may never have your friendship with Rob like you used to." He shot my heart with a dose of reality.

Of all the people in the entire world I could least stand losing, Dr. Nelson informed me I may in fact have lost Rob.

I don't believe him. I can't tell him that because he won't believe me either. He may know a lot about psychology, but he doesn't know how close Rob and I were. I think Rob's just been busy with his studies and sports. I think he's dating Dawnell too, so that's probably why he can't spend as much time with me. He probably thinks I need time to exercise and study, too. I'm sure our friendship will return the way it was. I'd made up my mind and convinced myself.

Persistent, I continued calling Rob and asking him if he'd like to go out for pizza or get together and talk or play pool or cards, like we used to.

"Nah, I can't tonight, Mart, because I have to help my Mom," he would say.

Determined to patch up our friendship, I persisted with phone calls. Occasionally, Rob would visit or ask if I would like to sit with him and a group of our friends at a girls basketball game. I accepted, but our communication at games was bland and infrequent. I felt our friendship dying a slow painful death, but I did everything in my power to keep it alive.

Not a day passed when I didn't struggle physically, emotionally, mentally or spiritually. My body still hurt, and as I looked up on my bedroom wall and saw Jesus hanging on the cross, I began to identify with him and the pain he might have felt when he gave his life up for every soul on the planet.

My pain can't compare to what you must've gone through, I said, kneeling beside my bed, gazing at the crucifix. I don't know about you, Jesus, but if it were me, I don't think I would've done what you did. I mean, you know what I went through, but it was like I almost didn't have a choice. It just happened. You had a choice, and you suffered for everyone...for me.

As I spoke to Jesus on the cross, the pain in my own body vanished. A transformation had begun, yet one I couldn't understand, not until I turned around and read the plaque on the opposite wall.

FOOTPRINTS

One night a man had a dream. He dreamed he was walking along the beach with the Lord. Across the sky flashed scenes from his life. For each scene, he noticed two sets of footprints in the sand; one belonged to him and the other to the Lord.

When the last scene of his life passed before him, he looked back at the footprints in the sand. He noticed that many times along the path of his life, there was only one set of footprints. He also noticed that it happened to be at the very lowest and saddest times in his life.

This really bothered him and he questioned the Lord about it. "Lord, you said that once I decided to follow you, you'd walk with me all the way. But I have noticed that during the most troublesome times in my life, there is only one set of footprints. I don't understand why when I needed you most, you would leave me."

The Lord replied: "My precious, precious child. I love you and would never leave you. During your times of trial and suffering when you see only one set of footprints, it was then that I carried you."

I stirred inside. My body, nervous. My mind, a kaleidoscope of senseless meaning.

Well c'mon, God! Why can't You help me?!! Don't You know I'm down here suffering? That's me walking the beach. That one set of footprints is mine— not Yours! I can't even walk without a handicap device. There's three indentations in the sand I'm walking on. If I can't ever run again as fast as I could before the accident, or if I can't get into college because I'm not smart enough, or if I can't do anything else I was able to do before my accident, it isn't my fault!!

Carry me? Right Lord. Are you going to carry me through these last weeks of school? What about finals? Do You have all the answers? Are You going to carry me up to the podium to receive my diploma? Maybe then I'll believe You're carrying me.

The anger and inner conflict built up a creative tension inside me, which a majority of world-renowned artists,

composers and poets literally thrived on in order to pro-
duce their masterpieces.

In search of an outlet for my anger, I reached for a
pen and wrote out on a piece of paper:

You said ask and I'll receive
So I asked and now I wait
You said it will happen in Your time
But in mine, You're much too late

How long will You ignore my life
I need Your love and grace
"How can't You see my hurt inside
Or the tears that stream my face

I pray a million times a day
You answer less than few
I'm ashamed to say I'm filled with faith
For who'd believe it's true?

Sometimes I feel You're artificial
It seems like You don't care
Sometimes when I'm alone at night
I'm certain You're not there

I'm sad, I weep, I'm broken down
I'm ridden with despair
I can't walk alone, my life's too tough
Or is that why You're there?

Again, no pain, all hurt erased. I had focused my
attention and expended my energy, even my anger, out
at the man on the cross. I held him responsible, not for

the accident, but for not helping me, as I wanted. I reread the poem I wrote, looked up at the crucifix and felt a calmness from within.

There must be some explanation for all this, I whispered to myself in attempt to understand my internal feelings. I wonder if priests and nuns always feel this serene. They're always close to You because they have to be. It's in their job description. Can You make me feel this way all the time, although I'm not a priest or nun? Life would be easier to handle, I think.

I looked around the room, suspicious of being watched. Then, I reached for a rosary on the shelf.

Here's something I can attach these kinds of feelings to. So if I carry this around with me in my pocket and I put my hand in and touch the small wooden beads and metal cross, could You bring me the feelings of peace and calmness? The cross on the wall is too big to put into my pocket, so this'll have to do, I said, talking to Christ.

◆   ◆   ◆

"Mart," Dad called from the family room where he sat in his regular spot on the couch. "I've been looking at these papers you brought home, and I see you're doing pretty good in most of your classes. You got an A in speech so far, which is terrific. Data processing is B, above average. Psychology and English are right up there as well. But the one I'm kind of worried about is this math class. They've got you in trigonometry, and it doesn't seem as though you're handling this too well."

I fooled myself believing nobody would notice my poor performance in math. The joke was over. I had to face the truth.

"Dad," I lowered my head, ashamed of my grades on trig tests and homework assignments, "I've been trying as hard as I can. I go to class everyday. I study every night. And I even go to math tutoring. In study hall, I spend more time trying to learn and remember trigonometry than anything else," I cried, but not because I felt sorry for myself, but because I remembered how I could feel my brain straining to perform certain functions of trig, yet couldn't make the connection.

"I see," Dad said, identifying more with the objective statements as opposed to feelings. "I don't doubt you are spending all the time you say you are on it, because I know how good a mathematician you are. I'm just concerned about the grade they're going to give you and whether or not they'll pass you. Because you know you need to pass in order to graduate on time."

Like a hermit in Siberia, I felt alone and frozen. Only I froze with fear. The promise I made to Dad, "I'm going to win, too," echoed in my mind. Nowhere to run. Nowhere to hide. Trigonometry, I told myself, had put me on my own one-yard line on fourth down and in need of a touchdown.

A rush of rationalization convinced me a June graduation ceremony was possible, at first.

I'm making good grades in all classes but math. I spend one hour a day, five days a week in class. That's five hours a week. I'm in tutoring two or three times a week for another hour each day. Let's call that another three hours. I spend at least two hours each night studying and doing my homework, times five nights a week, equals another ten hours. That's eighteen hours! That's got to be more than enough! But I don't get it. Even if I spend another twenty hours on it, it's not going to sink in. The only answer is: I can't do it!

Chapter 10

Nightfall after nightfall brought graduation day closer, like a guillotine blade sliding towards my neck.

I wished I were back in the hospital so I wouldn't have to go through with this, I thought, fighting to escape the here-and-now.

I slept at night with my right hand under my pillow, clenched in a fist, holding onto my rosary. I woke in the morning upon a tear-soaked pillow, after a night of tears of fear. The odds didn't favor me. I was David fighting Goliath, but in my hand I held not a slingshot, but a rosary. A handful of hope.

God, I can't see You, but I know You can hear me. Don't ask me how I know, because I don't know how I know You know. You get the point. Maybe I don't even really know You can hear me. Maybe I'm just trying to convince myself, I talked up at the ceiling, hoping God would poke His head through to prove He had heard me.

No drywall fell.

I've got about a month and a half to pass trig class. Or else I need a miracle.

◆　　◆　　◆

Up and start, I clicked my stopwatch to begin timing leg exercises. By now, I was working sets of ten repetitions, but not up and down. Instead, I raised the leg on a forty-five degree angle and timed how long I could hold it. Two minutes was my goal. As I exercised, I watched the clock tick seconds off, nearing two minutes as I struggled to keep the leg elevated. "1:47, 1:48, 1:49, 1:50...UGH!" The leg collapsed on top of the right leg. My gluteus medius had become stronger, but I didn't dare let myself become complacent.

"Rest if you must, but don't quit, don't quit, don't quit!" The words of the poem played in my head like a broken record.

"Honey, why don't you take a rest?"

Mom peered around the corner in an attempt to save me from myself. "You've been at it awhile now."

"Mom, I have to do this. The doctor isn't here watching over me to make sure I do a certain number of repetitions. I'm out of rehab. And the longer I wait, the longer it'll take for me to recover," I said.

◆　　◆　　◆

Journal entry. Sunday, May 2—Exercised five sets of twenty-five. GREAT DAY, THE LIMP IS GONE! I'm still a long way off from where I want it to be, though. Right now I can walk without a limp. I'm a long way away from slam dunking a basketball. In fact, sometimes I just don't know if it'll ever be the same as it was before the accident. It's been ten months since the accident. When will I return to one hundred percent? Should I set myself a deadline? I feel okay, but until I'm back in as good a condition, I won't allow myself to be satisfied.

I'm going to cover a softball game for the Crier and go jogging afterward. I think that if I do the things I used to do before my accident, things will get better.

I called Rob, but he was out playing tennis. I wish I could've played doubles with him. Maybe he'll play against me this summer vacation, like we used to do.

I made plans. Prom, post prom, tennis in the summer, running races again, returning to a championship softball team. As days passed, my list grew longer, until I caught myself and realized I had jumped the starting gun: I hadn't cleared the trig hurdle yet.

Chapter 11

1s a taste of honey better than no taste at all? Elated a few days ago that the limp was gone, despair set in on Wednesday when it reappeared. Angry, I countered it and fought back by locking the cane up in the closet.

"I don't need you anymore!"

The next day at school, classmates appeared surprised to see me un-handicapped. "Hey, no more gimp," Craig, a star basketball player, shouted down the hall during passing period. "I see you finally got rid of the cane, Marty. Is that just temporary or is it gone for good?" asked Ken, an all-conference football player who started on the varsity team his freshman year.

"That's it. No more cane."

But still, I limped, just a bit.

I felt my pulse race as I neared the doorway into trig class. Mrs. Bailey motioned me over to her desk.

"I had a talk on the phone with your Dad," she said. "He was a little concerned about how you were doing in class. When class ends, come up to the front and talk with me. We'll have more time then."

Worried and wondering, I asked, "Is something wrong?"

"Nope. Nothing at all to worry about, Marty."

I sat at my desk in front of the class, where I chose to sit in all my classes when given a choice because the fewer the distractions there were from the point of my desk to the front of the blackboard, the lesser the chance I would be distracted and, therefore, the higher my concentration level would be. Nonetheless, "I talked with your Dad," and "There's nothing wrong," hung like a grand piano above my head the full fifty minutes of class.

There's got to be something wrong if she talked with Dad. Why would Dad talk with her if there was nothing wrong? And why would she need to talk after class with me about anything if nothing was wrong? It certainly couldn't be that I aced my last test, because I could hardly remember those blasted formulas we were taught. Maybe she wants me to take a summer class in math and will pass me in this class and let me graduate on time if and only if I take a class this summer. Maybe she'll allow me to do algebra problems on the final, instead of trig, because she knows I can do those better than trig. But on the other hand...

"Marty, do you understand how we did that?" Mrs. Bailey asked, redirecting my attention back on course.

"Huh? Oh, no, I'm sorry," I stumbled back. "I was just, uh, thinking about what we were talking about earlier and lost my attention. I'm sorry."

Admit the truth and you will not be held to blame. Mrs. Bailey understood.

The next half-hour of class was Chinese water torture. I tended the thoughts in my head, in sheer wonderment, over what she had talked with Dad about. Stepping back out of my own picture, I took an objective look at it.

Obviously, they talked about trig class, number one. Since Mrs. Bailey is the teacher of the class and she talked with my Dad, obviously the conversation centered on me. So if they talked about me and the class, the news must've been either good or bad. If the news was good, maybe it could've been about some improvement I had made since class began, because my short-term memory is a wee bit better. But I really haven't gotten very good grades. So maybe it's bad news, in which case it could be anything. "Marty hasn't shown much improvement, he'll never be able to perform functions in trig due to the brain damage, so we're going to give him a chance to pass the class by cleaning the teacher's office after school and help grade papers from freshman algebra class."

Nah, couldn't be anything like that.

Before I knew it, the bell blared and class was over. I waited until all students had left before I walked over to Mrs. Bailey's desk.

"Okay, Marty," she addressed me, shuffling through papers on her desk. "First, let me apologize for having said anything to you before class because I noticed it had

you thinking the entire hour long, and I know it was difficult for you to devote your attention to today's lecture.

"Anyway, I had a talk with your father because he
was concerned about how you are doing in class and
whether you were going to receive a passing grade, because he said you need to pass trigonometry in order to
graduate."

My innards trembled, forewarning the body of a possible earthquake. Nerves frazzled, eyes watered, heartbeat
pounded as if at an Indian pow-wow.

"I told your Dad, and this is something I haven't even
told you yet, that Dr. Manos, your guidance counselor,
and I had a conference in regard to your graduating on
time and that you needed to pass trigonometry in order
to graduate. Well, we've only got a few more weeks before the ceremony and, as I'm sure you're aware, you just
aren't pulling the grades you need in order to pass."

The cold, sharp edge of the guillotine was now resting on the back of my neck. It wouldn't be much longer.
My death sentence was written.

Go ahead, Mrs. Bailey. I'm not one who can hide
from the truth.

"So what I told your father is what Dr. Manos and I
agreed upon, and that's that you will get an E grade for
the course, which means you failed, but because of the
unusual circumstances, you will earn credit for the class."

I breathed a deep sigh of relief. Another miracle granted.

I've cleared my final hurdle. All that's ahead of me is
the finish line, I praised myself before engaging in a bout
of denial. Feeling as though I were out front of everyone,
empowered me only more so, and motivated me to run

harder and faster in the race of life. More confident about myself, I spent even more time trying to absorb all the formulas and notes I had taken in hope of surprising everyone, even myself, by scoring an A on the final exam.

I'll prove to them that I don't really need any free gift. I want to earn the passing grade on my own. I'll spend a lot of time reviewing all my notes and going to the tutor a few more times during the week. I'll learn all the formulas again and just keep practicing by working on problems. Like they say, "Practice makes perfect."

A C on my communications test and a C+ on my survey test. I don't think I'll ever really need to know who the leaders of Third World countries are or how to buy stock anyway, I persuaded myself to believe. I'll bet I can improve those grades when I take the final exam.

Never neglecting my exercise routine, I took a break from studying and fell down on the carpet, but this time with a feeling of complete lightness. No more elephants on my left leg. Rather, an overwhelming sense of oneness, with myself and Him.

I pushed hard and strained to keep my leg elevated when I saw the stopwatch nearing the two-minute mark. Although I knew the gluteus medius was getting stronger and my limp was diminishing, nothing was getting any easier. I had a long way to go.

Don't quit! Don't quit! Don't quit! Go for it! Win, win, win, win! I gasped for air as my leg dropped slowly when the stopwatch read two minutes. The closer two minutes neared on the watch, the more difficult it was to keep the leg up. A psychological thing. After completing my fourth of five sets of twenty-five for the day, I called up my friend Mike to the house to play tennis on the courts behind the house. Warm weather and an improved physical condition enabled me to enjoy additional exercise on a regular basis.

After a slow hour of tennis, Mom called me in. "Marty, telephone call!"

Who was it? I wondered. Maybe Rob finally had enough time to think about all this and he wants to continue our friendship. Or maybe it's Fr. Greg.

"Hello, Marty, this is Corrine, Jeannette's friend."

"Oh, hi, Corrine. Hold on just a minute and I'll see if Jeannette is here," I said, not realizing her reason for calling.

"No, Marty, wait a minute. I called you," she said, catching me by surprise. She never called me before. Thoughts rushed through my mind as to why she would be calling me. I couldn't figure it out.

"I was talking with Jeannette in class and she said you hadn't asked any girl to senior prom yet, but that you wanted to go."

My faced turned tomato-red with embarrassment. I, a senior, felt ashamed I was failing to meet one of the highest obligations of every senior: attend senior prom. I felt as if St. Peter were on the opposite side of the telephone checking up on me, catching me off guard.

"I, uh, well, I mean I was, um..." quickly accessing my mental file of excuses, I fumbled through an assortment of 'I can't because...' reasons, but offered the best excuse I knew. "Corrine, I'd like to go to senior prom, but I have nobody to go with. I haven't been dating any girls senior year because I stayed home first semester, and I didn't have any time to date second semester because I had to continue rehabilitation on my leg and spend a lot of extra time on my studies. I didn't think it was right to ask any of the girls in my class because everybody I know who is going to prom has been going steady with their guy. So I guess I was just going to let it go. I figure I still have senior breakfast," I confessed, worming my way out of embarrassment.

"Marty, I'd like to be your date if you'd like to go," she asked.

Jeannette told her to ask me because she feels sorry for me. That's why Corrine called, I thought, feeling belligerent toward my baby sister, instead of accepting it as an act of love. If I turn Corrine down, I'll put myself to shame because she knows I don't have a date and she'll think I'm a jerk because she's made me an offer to save me from senior year shame of missing prom and I'll have turned her down.

A quiet, gentle girl, Corrine was someone I didn't have half a heart to turn down.

"Yes, I'd like to go with you, Corrine," I accepted her invitation, yet felt a definite role-reversal had occurred through our interaction.

I couldn't bear standing up to friends at school when the topic of prom arose and admitting, "Oh, yeah, I'll be there all right. Corrine asked me to go."

C'mon, Folan, a girl asking a guy to prom. You're the one who does the asking—not the woman.

I'll tell them she's a friend of mine and we decided to go together, that's all.

"I'll be so happy to go with you. I'm sure we'll have a great time," she said. "But there's just one thing. I won't be able to go to post prom because I have a doctor's appointment at the hospital and it's going to take more than just an hour."

After finalizing prom plans with her, I fished for a post-prom date, contacting Mike and a few other friends inquiring as to whether their dates had friends who would like to go to post prom, kind of like as a tag-a-long. The odds were against my finding an available girl at school, so I paged through my phone book and made a call.

"Carol? Hi, this is Marty. How are you doing?" I asked, the usual generic opening lines for phone calls. A former three-sport athlete at Conant whom I reported on since my freshman year, Carol would be any guy's dream date: intelligent, athletic, overflowing with kindness and concern and a great listener, all the perfect qualities packaged in the most beautiful, lovely appearance any guy would desire in his girl.

After catching up on the past two years and explaining to Carol my particular prom predicament, I popped the question: "So I was wondering if you would like to go to post prom, Carol?"

I'd let it out. There was no taking it back, I trembled with fear of rejection, as if I'd just proposed to marry her.

"Sure! I'd love to go! It'll be great going to a post prom again two years after I graduated," she laughed, amused with the opportunity.

Relieved I had found dates for prom and post prom, my nerves buzzed as final exams and graduation day approached. I smiled at the senior citizens who worked as hall monitors at school. I'd become friends with a few through my mishap, and they expressed feelings of fulfillment over having assisted me and developed a friendship with me. I reciprocated the feelings. As I walked through the halls, however, a mysterious feeling overtook me. I sensed my presence at Conant beyond the current year. Something was telling me I would find myself walking these same halls in the future.

Oh, God, don't tell me I'm not going to graduate on time and it'll be necessary to take classes this summer, I trembled with fear at the realistic possibility.

That night in bed, I had a dream:

> Five hundred and seven of us seniors stood outside the fence by the football field in our blue gowns and caps with red and white trim, waiting to file in to begin the commencement ceremony. A hand softly gripped my shoulder from behind.
>
> "Marty, would you come with me so we can talk for a moment." It was Dr. Manos. I turned and followed him back into the school and walked behind him down the main hall, as if being led to an execution chamber. Screams of silence echoed throughout the corridor. As we neared the executive office, Dr. Manos' pace slowed down to a funeral march up to his doorway. Turning slowly to face me, he spoke to me in a soft voice. "Go in and have a seat at the table."

As I stepped towards the table, I limped heavily, as if trying to remind Dr. Manos of my plight and beg for his mercy.

He didn't sit down. Instead, he walked to the eight-foot high file cabinet and searched the alphabetical arrangement to find my folder. Fearful of what he would say to me, I tried to calm my nerves by remembering how I felt when Mrs. Bailey and Corrine spoke to me and that they delivered news of relief and happiness.

Somehow, I knew Dr. Manos' announcement would differ.

"Marty, I'm going to get to the point with you. You didn't pass all of your classes, therefore, you won't be graduating tonight," he said.

The room temperature dropped. I felt a damp clamminess on my hands and face. Then, before my eyes, Dr. Manos vanished. Blackness filled the room as the lights burned out instantly. Left in a cold, dark cellar of doom. Alone, robbed of all hope. I fell to the floor and screamed, "Please let me go! Just give me a chance, Dr. Manos!"

I awoke in bed, again, upon a wet pillow soaked with my tears, like so many times before.

Sunday in church, another piece of my puzzle fit in place as Fr. Greg read from the Gospel of Matthew (2:13).

"After they had left, an angel of the Lord appeared in a dream to Joseph and said, 'Get up, take the child and his mother and run away to Egypt, and stay there until I tell you to leave. Herod will be looking for the child to kill him."

As I listened to the story, my heart and mind became flushed with fear that my dream was somehow a message from God.

Angels speak to people in their dreams. God sends them to deliver messages to people. If he sent an angel to tell Joseph to take the child and his wife and escape to Egypt, maybe my dream was a message forewarning me of my future. God wouldn't want me to be shocked on graduation day when I'd be the only one left on the football field without a diploma. So maybe He's saving me the embarrassment by warning me in a dream to be prepared. Maybe it's a message to study a lot harder.

Later in the afternoon as I sat down at the kitchen table to study, I recalled the mysterious feeling I had when I talked with the hall monitors, when I sensed my presence at Conant beyond the current school year. All signs pointed one way: Back to School. You won't graduate on time.

It doesn't make any sense! How is it I won't be able to graduate on time if they're going to give me an E in trig and I'm getting passing grades in all my other classes? The dream is wrong! It's a nightmare, not a message from God to be prepared for the greatest shock of my life, when I walk up to receive my diploma and get handed a return ticket back into school instead. It's wrong! You're all wrong! I'm going to graduate on time, I shouted, still quivering with fear.

The weeks raced by. I chose not to consult Dr. Nelson about my dream and fear of not graduating. To do so would be to admit to myself my doubts I'd graduate on time.

Mid-semester I had met with Mrs. Weisner, my guidance counselor, about choosing a college to attend. Advised, at the time, that opting for junior college courses to start off with would be more favorable for my parents and myself, I compromised. Knowing it was almost every student's dream to fly the bird's nest and move away to begin life anew at a university, I agreed to fill out registration forms for Harper Jr. College, a few miles down the street from my family's home, only if I could apply to Blackburn College, a small school of five-hundred plus students in Carlinville, Illinois, where Cindy studied. If I wasn't accepted at Blackburn, I'd attend Harper.

Mom and Dad hadn't discussed college with me. Completing high school carried with it enough distress. Repeatedly, I assured myself I would attend and graduate from college, somewhere, someday.

As days sped by, college didn't appear any closer than around the corner and far in the distance. It remained a dormant thought which hung at the edge of my mind due to the strain exam preparation put on me.

Thinking had been a laborious chore since the accident. My mental file cabinet containing all the knowledge I had collected on so many subjects through the years and tools of thought paradigms had been closed and locked since my brain injury. My ability to freely access information had been impaired. Now I had to stop, think about what I wanted to know and attempt to unlock the cabinet and sort through folders to find information, which meant rerouting my brain to trace back down the memory channel and search for the original seeds of information. Through the past ten months, constant reruns back down the path gradually improved the retrieval process. But still, any condition which I deemed sub-par to that of my pre-accident state was entirely unsatisfactory.

Monday was the turn into the home stretch, the last full week before graduation and the week of prom.

"The final exam is one hundred sixty questions, all multiple choice," said Ms. Blatt, my senior social survey teacher. "Take your time because you'll have more than enough to complete it."

"You won't," a devil on my shoulder told me, as I froze with fear. "There's no way you're going to be able to remember all that information about politics and stock markets and leaders of Third World countries and who led battles during the wars and who all those inventors were and..." Flick. The devil flew off my shoulder with the quick movement of my thumb and forefinger. I melted all fear with my fires of determination to pass the exam with flying colors.

The final quarter grades posted on the outside of the door before class boosted my spirits. I had earned a B, which would not change, unless I either aced or flunked the final.

Each exam I handed in brought me one step closer to receiving my diploma, I felt. Ironically, however, I saw no white light at the end of my tunnel. Instead, each step pulled me deeper into darkness. The trig exam waited for me seventh hour.

Too nervous to eat lunch fifth hour, I walked outside, sat on the bench and bargained with the Heavenly Board.

"God, I've got a plan for how we can work this out," I whispered aloud, looking up at the sky, hoping to see Him move a cloud out of the way as a signal that I had His attention. "I know You've got some angels up there with You, several teams of them, I'll bet, and I was thinking that since You know everything, including what the answers on the trig test are, maybe You could tell a few of Your angels and send them down upon my shoulder while I'm taking the test so they could see whether or not I'm answering the questions correctly.

"I'm not asking You to have them give me the answers," I quickly assured Him, escaping the slightest notion of cheating. "I just want it so that if I don't answer a question correctly, maybe they could jump on my shoulder or tug on my ear or give me some kind of sign. That way I'd know the answer was wrong and I could do it all over again. I wouldn't be cheating because they wouldn't give me any answers. I think that's a fair plan, don't You? I mean, it makes it a little bit easier on You because it's not like I'm asking You for another miracle. Just a little assistance."

The sun ran out from behind the clouds and beamed a bright eighty-degree smile on my face. I knew God had answered me.

I asked in prayer and believed He'd answer, like so many times before; so I had no reason to twitch even a muscle during exam hour.

The square root of co-sine over pi plus or minus negative square root of nine pi squared is greater than or equal to...I don't get it, I whispered. It can't be (D) all of the above, or (C) both A and B, so it has to be either (A) or

(B). Hey, angel, I beckoned him quietly, hoping to feel a gentle movement of my pencil to either (A) or (B).

I squeezed my eyelids tightly and pleaded beneath my breath for divine intervention, waiting...waiting...waiting for my No. 2 pencil to move.

Yeah, yeah, oh yeah, I can feel it, I whispered wordlessly to myself with a broad smile, breathing in and out as in a deep meditative state. I blindly stuck the lead tip on (B) and colored it in.

I thanked the mathematical angel and proceeded to the next problem. The odds of passing the sixty problem exam favored me highly, according to my own self-designed master plan for test taking: (1) Read the problem; (2) Try to solve it prior to looking at the multiple-choice answers; (3) If not possible, look at selection of answers; (4) Eliminate obvious wrong answers; (5) Plug each remaining answer into the problem; (6) If still have not arrived at an answer, ask the angel.

Chapter 12

"**F**inally, it's over, Jamaal," I told a classmate at my locker. "I finished my last exam in trig class, but I'm not as relieved as I thought I'd be. I feel more sadness than anything. It's like a funeral because the coffin was nailed shut after I handed in my last exam, and here after four years together, we're all going our separate ways and will probably never see most of our friends again, except for ten years from now when everybody returns for the class reunion."

"You're sad, man?" Jamaal jeered at me in his brotherly language. "Shoot, bro, I be looking ahead to this moment since the day I walk in this here place. Know what I mean? It ain't too cool or nothing, like I mean you and me, man, you know how we always talk at our lockers and been friends since freshman year and all? Yeah, I sad 'bout that too, Marty, but hey, there be better things out there in the world soon as we leave this place, you dig?"

I smiled, knowing in honesty that no matter how far apart friends may be, a special part of each always remains with the other.

"Yeah, I dig you, man," I said, slapping hands ritualistically. "Better things out there for you and me."

Chapter 13

Upon returning home, I found a letter from Rob in an envelope on my dresser:

Marty,

In case you haven't noticed, I haven't been returning any of your phone calls. I know it's been a long time since we really talked, but that's simply because I'm not ready yet. And that's why I haven't returned any calls, because I wasn't ready, but now I am. I guess I'll just start from the beginning and see if I can try to explain this whole mess.

You see, while you were in the hospital, I had a lot of time to think about things. I thought about all the good times we had, the things we used to do, and generally just about us. I was pretty stunned after we identified you. To tell you the truth, we weren't sure whether you were going to live or die. However, I knew that you were going to live. You see, it wasn't you alone that was in that accident, it was both of us. We were so close, that when you hit that jeep, you felt the physical pain and I felt the emotional and mental pain. Someday, you'll be able to forget entirely what happened that day, because by then, physically you'll be back to normal. But I'll never be able to forget entirely what happened that day. I'll have everything that happened that summer planted in my brain for the rest of my life. I have, however, resolved never to let something like that happen again. Never again will I let someone so close and dear to me come so close to dying. How? Simple. I have decided never to become as close to anybody as I was with you. That is the main reason why our friendship will never be the same as it was. I hope that answers the questions you've had on your mind.

Still friends, (but not the same),

Rob

P.S. I know what you're thinking. Right now you're saying to yourself, "How can he throw away all those good times we had and our special friendship just like that?" The answer is, I can't. Which is why I try to put all those things out of my mind as much as possible. That's also why I sometimes cry at night and ask God why things have to be this way.

Why do things have to be this way? The question had resounded in my head every day since the accident. I never found an answer. Not in the Bible. Not in any profound teachings of any gurus, mystics or preachers.

The truth is there is no answer to the question. As soon as we can first accept that, the sooner it will be that we can then work through the predicaments we are in. But never a moment before.

Damnit, Rob. Had I spent the past nine months on my back asking why things had to be this way, instead of facing the fact that this is the way it is, I'd never have made it this far.

Sure, I've had doubts and I've asked questions. But if you let your doubts and inquiries paralyze you and halt your progress toward your goal, then you'll never reach your goal. Plain and simple.

Chapter 14

Mom and Dad radiated a proud parental glow in the living room at home where Dad set up his camera to shoot one of several thousand pictures parents would take of their sons and daughters on graduation night. A moment in the life of any boy or girl which would never be forgotten.

"Just a little bit to the right, and Mom, you put your arms around him just like that and hold it..." said chief photographer Dad, who had taken tens of thousands of slide pictures since he married Mom. And once a year, usually with a houseful of company, he'd pull the screen out from the closet, plug in the projector and show slides for hours. Better than the announcer for a National Geographic documentary, or a Public Broadcasting Corporation special, Dad would narrate the stories of his travels across the world; including his visits to Morocco, the honeymoon fishing trip with Mom in Michigan where he caught a trout, for which he was so proud of himself that he provided everyone watching the slides with historical information on various types of fish; the birth of his three children; holidays; and anything else worth recording on film to store in the Folan family archives.

Tonight's my story, if they really do hand me my diploma. Some afternoon when friends and neighbors gather round the table in the Folan house and Dad sets up the projector, I'll take over the storytelling when he beams my picture on the screen.

"It was a hot and sunny afternoon," I'll begin my story.

At that moment I felt the warm embracing glow of Mom and Dad's pride in having brought me up. Tonight is their night of recognition and honor as much as it is mine. If I come home tonight with my diploma, they will be more highly honored than I. There isn't any other parent who will be there tonight who can possibly feel as successful and proud as my Mom and Dad.

"Now let's get one of you and Dad together," Mom said, taking the camera from Dad. As he walked over to me and put his arm around my shoulder, I felt love.

Seated in chairs on the football field, five hundred and six classmates waited patiently. I, however, couldn't sit still. Certain of their status once their names were called, boys and girls in the class would accept their diplomas as a ticket either to a university, trade school or full-time job. My ticket could be a Chance card: Go Back to High School, Do Not Pass Up Education, Do Not Collect Your Diploma. And back around the board I'd go, striving to meet the requirements set by the state and catch up on other players, who will have furthered their education at college, adding power to their lives, like buying property and adding hotels and houses in the game.

The class valedictorian had spoken and Dr. Manos and other administrators began handing out diplomas, shaking hands as each student's name was read. My row stood up.

My Lord, this could be the most embarrassing moment of my life if I get to the front and they don't hand me a diploma. Mom and Dad would be devastated. Please don't let there be any mistake, I begged, holding my breath each step of the way. Maybe they won't give it to me because I didn't heed their advice and drop a few classes and graduate after summer school. I hope they aren't mad at me.

"Jodie Fell, Michael Felten, Charles Finch, Robert Fitch," the names were called in order. I felt myself being led to the edge of a cliff. If my name wasn't read, over I'd go, falling, falling, falling...all the way. If they did read my name, upward I'd soar like a dove, far and away beyond the horizon, above the clouds, so light and free and into a new future!

"...Martin Folan," Dr. Manos called my name, handed me my golden certificate and shook my hand. Unlike every other parent seated in the stands, my parents, Cindy and Jeannette rose to their feet and clapped and cheered wildly. I turned to them, held up my diploma with tears running down my cheeks, waved at them and smiled.

Chapter 15

"Oh, Mart, I'm so proud of you," Cindy hugged me in the kitchen back home.

"You deserved it, honey, after all you've been through," Mom said, lighting the candles on a chocolate frosted cake set on the table.

Jeannette's face lit up when she looked at me, proud to have a brother ahead of her in school in whose footsteps she would follow. As neighbors and relatives walked into the house for the celebration, I excused myself and walked into my bedroom where I looked up at the plaque on the wall and saw footprints in the sand, the footprints that had carried me on an eleven-month journey from the hospital, through the fires of a living hell and up to the podium to receive my award. I cried tears of thanks for what I never could've accomplished on my own.

I returned to the kitchen to the handshakes and hugs of those who had seen me through it all. Many handed me cards and gifts. I overheard talk in the background about college.

"I don't know what his plans are," a neighbor whispered to my aunt. "I don't think he's going to college right away. Maybe he'll take some time off first."

"My boy went," Mrs. Brazel said to Mom, "and he said, 'Mom, college is much different from high school. It's ten times as hard, and some days I just feel like packing my bags and coming home.'"

Mom responded. "Well, he's been so busy with trying to get all his work done so he could graduate on time that I don't even think he's had a chance to talk to his guidance counselor at school about college. He needs some time off to work on his leg anyway. And I'm sure when he's ready to start school, he can take some courses at Harper and stay at home until he's ready to go to a bigger school."

"Excuse me," I spoke above the conversations to make an announcement. "I couldn't help but overhear the talk about college and how difficult it's been for Jim and Susie and everyone else. Getting through high school alone was a huge mountain for me to climb, so I can identify with you who have kids in college.

"I spoke with my guidance counselor about college and sent an application to Harper," I said, which caused a few people to whisper. "But I also sent one to Blackburn College, where my sister Cindy is going, and that is where I will begin my college education this fall."

Everyone was surprised. Jaws dropped and eyes lit up, as if they themselves had discovered Jesus missing from the tomb. Mom and Dad seem stunned. Cindy ran up to me, wrapped her arms around me and congratulated me.

"Oh, Mart, I'm so happy for you. We'll have a great time there. I'll show you everything and introduce you to everybody and if you need anything, you know I'll be there to help."

"Mom and Dad," I called to their attention as I walked over to them, "I know I didn't talk with you about this earlier, but I discussed this with Mrs. Weisner and sent applications out from her office. I thought about Harper, but reconsidered schools when I knew that Cindy was at Blackburn, which is a very small school, hence there won't be a lot of walking around campus. I think it has only five hundred students or so, and she knows most of them by now, so if I had any troubles, I could always rely on her. And I'm just going there to get started. I don't plan on graduating from there because they don't offer journalism as a major. I'm taking general education classes my first year."

My explanation eased their nerves, somewhat.

"College is a lot harder, Marty," Mom said, nervous about my decision. "I wish you would've talked with Dad and me about this first. I'm not saying we don't want you to go to school. It's just that you kind of caught us off guard. And like Mrs. Brazel said, her son Rick is having a very difficult time at college, and he didn't go through what you did. I just think it would be better for you to take it easy to begin with."

The room fell silent, as everyone focused in on the center of the kitchen where I stood in front of the lighted graduation cake. I looked at all twenty-four faces, turned around, then blew out each and every candle.

"Mom and Dad...I just want a chance."

When a new day dawns
God takes away our yesterday
And with this, our thoughts, words and actions
But we will always carry our memories
Memories of good and bad will live on in our
minds
Many times, we wish they were gone
But forever they will live on
So must we find strength to go on living
Each new day as it comes
Not knowing what's ahead of us,
Yet having the will to carry on
And leave our yesterdays behind.
           — Jeannette

Chapter 16

Brothers and Sisters in Christ,

Thank you for taking this journey with me through the most painful experience of my life. I am grateful for the friends, family and those whom I did not know very well, who lifted me up in prayer as well as provided me with their company, emotional and physical support, and love. People came forth to help me each in their own ways. Many of them with whom I had deeper and more personal relations embraced me and suffered with me from day one onward. My mother listed the names of everyone who visited me at the two hospitals throughout the 69 days. Some visitors were mere acquaintances but cared enough to pay me a visit. To this day, I carry them deep in my heart.

As I look back at my accident and the seemingly endless period of recovery and rehabilitation, I once again turn to my mother and father and thank them for raising me as they did. My parents were the sowers of seeds in my life. "Let's kneel down before bed and pray." To thank God for all that my family has been given, however simple it may be. And ask God to bless Mom and Dad and my sisters, and the dog, along with my aunts, uncles, all my cousins and my grandmas and grandpas. And to pray for protection of my family's home.

My parents taught me how to pray as a child, but I discontinued my nighttime ritual shortly after I'd begun. God became once a week for an hour on Sundays, and Christmas, Easter, and Holy Days. Mom and Dad tried again, however, when they placed a copy of *A Catholic Prayer Book*, by Fr. Robert Fox, (Our Sunday Visitor) in my Easter basket when I was ten years old. At first, I only used it as a reference prayer book for times when I needed for God to hear me. For instance, when I needed to boost my grades at school and the big exam neared, I turned to the table of contents and looked up, "A Student's Prayer Before a Test." I prayed, then put the book back on the shelf. Years later when I began dating, I fell in love with Mary McMahon my sophomore year of high school. Before my dates with her, I'd page through to another special prayer, "A Boy's Prayer Before a Date."

God fit in where I wanted Him and stayed out of my life otherwise. Perfectly convenient, until July 10, 1981, when my life changed and I became a different person. Prayer became a central part of my life. In fact, during my weeks in the hospitals, I recited Fr. Fox's "Night Prayer" every evening from then until now.

NIGHT PRAYER

Thank You, dear God, for the graces of this day. I have not served You perfectly and yet You have preserved and protected me unto this moment. I renew the offering I made of my total self this morning. I offer You too whatever sins I have committed this day so that they may be washed away in the most precious blood of my Lord and Savior, Jesus Christ.

(Reflect on your sins of the day. What caused them? How could you have prevented such sin? What will you do in the future to avoid such sin?)

Dear Lord, natural sleep is a figure of the sleep of death. Some day shall be my last day on earth. Then I will go to my true and eternal home in heaven. Please make me ready for that last day on earth and my first day in eternity.

My soul waits for the Lord. I trust in His word. Out of the depths I cry to You, O Lord. Lord, hear my voice. I trust in You, O my God.

Sacred Heart of Jesus, please have mercy on my poor soul. Immaculate Heart of Mary, intercede with your Son to bestow His love and grace upon me.

As the great woman of faith, O Mary, as Mother of the Church, keep me always loyal and true in the knowledge and practice of my holy Catholic faith.

Angels of heaven, watch over me this night.
My guardian angel, keep my soul holy and pure
this night through your intercessory power. St.
Martin, my patron saint, please intercede for
me that I may be brought safely home one day.
I ask this all through Christ, my Lord.
Amen.

My parents raised me the best they could and de-
serve a special place in heaven because of their love. We
were a middle-class family who had enough to get along.
As children, however, my sisters and I knew we had more
than our fair share. Although far from spoiled, we were
never without. Family meals, for instance, were special at
the Folan home for a few reasons. Frozen foods and TV
dinners were quarantined from our house. All meals were
homemade by both Mom and Dad. No dry cereal or
fried eggs with toast at our house on the weekends. Dad
prepared gourmet breakfasts every Saturday and Sunday
until my sisters and I moved out on our own, but not without his recipes in hand. Dad created some of the wildest
entrees. Brown scrambled eggs was my favorite. Mixed
in with three eggs and milk were douses of barbecue sauce,
level teaspoons of curry powder with a pinch of thyme, a
dash of paprika, and some salt. Not so strong that it kicked
you between the eyes at your first meal of the day, but
too potent for the tender tummies of Mom, Cindy and
Jeannette.

Then, a dish so eye-appealing that most artists couldn't
replicate it with their paint brushes. Puff Eggs. Very carefully, Dad would separate the egg whites from yolks, beat

the whites in a bowl with cream of tartar and other spices until they formed peaks, like a meringue. On pieces of bread, he'd spread the fluff mix, then carve out a hole in the center with a knife. Back to the yolks, without breaking them, he'd gently slip them into the center of the fluff on the bread. It took an extremely steady hand, because if the yolk broke on the sharp edge of the eggshell, the recipe was ruined. Dad would usually make six puff eggs at a time. With all six on a baking sheet, he'd pop them into the oven until the peaks turned golden brown. Served with cinnamon sprinkled bacon and a glass of orange juice, the meal was one of many inscrutably delicious morning feasts. Also on his list of gourmet entrees was cheese soufflé and poached eggs on English muffin with ham and generous ladles full of cheese sauce.

Breakfast excited Jeannette, Cindy, and me for another reason also: the orange juice race.

"Hands on your glasses. Are you ready?" Dad would ask, his hand tightly gripping his glass. "Are you set? Go!"

Whoever gulped down their OJ and set their glass down first was the winner. Usually it was Dad, until junior high school.

Since early childhood, music has played throughout my life, even Saturday mornings. As Dad prepared our meals, he would sing along with ballads played on WOPA's Irish Hour with Jack Haggerty. *Whiskey in the Jar, Wild Colonial Boy, When Irish Eyes are Smiling* and other Irish ballads he'd sing out from the kitchen while dancing an Irish jig. Breakfasts were forever a weekend ritual at the Folan house.

Mom took pride in her cooking as well, though she'd never show it. "Oh, I just threw something together because I didn't know what to make tonight," she'd tell us before serving scrumpdillicious meals. Even after hours of preparation of the Sunday afternoon feast, where we would have over for company Nana and Papa, Aunt Hinkie, Uncle Eddie and Peter, Tim, Mary Ellen and Nancy, we'd no sooner complete the clockwise serving rotation of roast beef with mushroom gravy, creamed green beans, sweet potatoes with marshmallows on top, mashed potatoes, rolls and various other side dishes when Mom would nonchalantly say, "The meat might be a little tough. I probably should have kept it in a little longer," or "Oh, these potatoes are lumpy." Or last but not least, the I-don't-know-what's-wrong-with-it-but-there's-something-wrong statement.

"Pass the meatloaf, please," I'd ask, at a typical weeknight dinner, hungry for more. "This is good, Mom."

"Well, it's okay, but I don't know. It just didn't come out the way I wanted."

"How did you want it to come out, Mom? It's meatloaf," I'd remind her.

When I sat down for dinner, I entered my father's territory, a ring of discipline and rules. Vegetables were my nemesis. Whether it was broccoli, carrots, Brussels sprouts, green beans, unless they were creamed, or the arch-nemesis, spinach. Nothing, I mean absolutely nothing, was any worse in the world than for my tongue to feel the slimy clump of green seaweed and my taste buds to be awakened by the awful taste of a bitter metallic explosion of chlorophyll. Spinach was a form of punishment for me, the most severe. What was worse, I never deserved it. But there I would sit at the table, like a Christian thrown into the center of the coliseum to be devoured by a lion, watching Dad. Normally on those nights when Mom would serve some loathsome, putrid vegetable, Dad would fetch his most recently purchased paperback book and return to the table to read. With every turn of the page, he would raise his eyes, look down at my plate and glance back up at me and telegraph the message: "EAT NOW!"

I figured there had to be some way for the Christian to flee the grasp of the savage lion and escape from the coliseum. If he could jump into the spectaculum, or even run around and tire out the lion, his life would be saved. But the lion stared his prey down and saw for itself a thick, juicy piece of human dinner. Tasty tasty.

Dad glanced up again as he turned another page. The Christian would surely be doomed, I'd figured, but I knew I had a chance. I decided to take the coup de grace of all risks. Meticulously with my fork, I scooped up a clump of cold spinach, twirled it on the fork, as if it were spaghetti, to collect as much as possible, then, speedily, I stuffed the frozen soggy turf into my mouth. A planned choke response followed, then I swept my hand to the left for a napkin. Automatically, my paper catcher's mitt caught the speedy green ball of food, which flew out of my mouth faster then a Nolan Ryan fastball. Still with a feigned choke, I ran into the bathroom. All I needed to complete the scene was fake vomit.

Once I'd reached my safety zone, I dropped the non-odorous napkin into the john and flushed. Mission accomplished. Judges score: 5, due to the motherlode of spinach remaining on my plate. Dad knew I'd return to eat it. He'd conceded once, but once was enough.

Back into the coliseum. The Christian best roll over and play dead, I thought. There's simply no way out. Colder now, the spinach had begun to form ice crystals.

"Dad, did you put more on my plate?" I wanted only to hear his voice to know that he was still my father and not some mutant clone hired to administer severe disciplinary action due to my refusal to eat my vegetables.

"No, nothing on your plate has moved since you ran off to the bathroom," he said, in a gentle voice as he looked up from his book. "You only have another bite or two left, Mart. Then we'll see about some dessert. How about that?"

'How about that?'! I couldn't believe it! All I had to do was stomach the last piddly pile of Martian stew and I was home free. I psyched myself up. My mind had become an Indy speedway. The race cars were messages: 1) Just one more bite; 2) It's not really that bad; 3) Imagine the spinach is hot pizza; 4) Swallow and you've finished.

The cars raced round and round in my mind. Messages getting louder and louder. Then, car number five came out of nowhere and sped past the others to cross the finish line: "Mart, I've got some French vanilla ice cream for dessert."

Quicker than I could say 31 flavors, I shoveled the cold ball of flavor 32 into my mouth and gulped it down. Finished!

Dad's lesson regarding veggies was, "There are going to be some things in life you aren't going to want to do, but you'll have to do them. It's part of life." After my accident, those words echoed in my head every time I dropped my tired lame body down onto the hallway carpet to exercise my leg, or struggled to lift my left arm or, with futility, tried to reroute my brain's math wires to solve trigonometry problems.

Later on in life, when I set out on job hunts through help wanted ads, job agencies, computer listings, employee newsletters, temporary agencies, and permanent staffing agencies, I remembered those words of wisdom, "There are going to be some things in life you aren't going to want to do, but you'll have to do them. It's part of life." Like spend eight hours a day in search of a job so I could pay my bills, put gas in the car and live as normal an unemployed life as possible. It was part of life. It made me a stronger person. I'll probably need to conduct a job search sometime again in my life, too.

One of the most difficult "things" in life I've had to do since my accident was say my last good-byes at the gravesides of friends who were killed in their own accidents, or due to cancer or AIDS, or alcohol-related deaths. Thank You, Lord, for giving me a second chance.

◆　　◆　　◆

My mother was a professional piano and organ teacher. My sisters also developed not only their musical talents, but vocal as well. Dad played an accordion. I listened. I grew to love music. Piano concertos, Irish ballads, orchestral arrangements, quiet music, loud music, rock and pop and country. Even marching band music.

Then smooth jazz years later. I never took much to rap, though.

I've refined my tastes and sharpened my listening skills to where I no longer simply listen to music anymore. I experience it. I let myself roll around in the lyrics of a love song. I open myself up to music so that it plays within me, unceasingly. Throughout my life, music and melodies have lifted me, inspired me to extend myself so that I connect with others, to feel as though I could reach up and touch God in the sky. Music enables people to transcend boundaries of race, religion, gender, and political affiliations because the common language that is spoken and sung among all of us is music. Mac Davis sang a line in his song, *I Believe in Music:* Music is the universal language....

The crystal clear voice of Celine Dion, or the tender-hearted love songs that gently brush one's heart as Air Supply sings, or the rhythm and beat of Prince, AC-DC, and George Michael.

Nothing's Gonna Stop Us Now (Starship), *We are the Champions* (Queen), *Walking on Sunshine* (Katrina and the Waves), *Only the Strong Survive* (REO Speedwagon) *Feeling Stronger Everyday* (Chicago), *I Knew You Were Waiting (for Me)* (George Michael and Aretha Franklin) and *Ain't Nothin' Gonna Break My Stride* (Matthew Wilder) pump the mind with positive messages. Nothing but positive input.

◆   ◆   ◆

My parents always gave my sisters and me mountains of presents at Christmas, surprise birthday parties, new clothes when they were needed. But more than material goods, they gave me the encouragement and, more importantly, the drive to overcome life's hurdles. They gave me the opportunities to try and try and try again, when I pleaded for a second chance, whether with grades, or sports, or misbehaviors. Most of all, my parents gave me unconditional love. No matter how mischievous or wrong I might have been, when I knew that if I were in their shoes, I wouldn't even forgive myself, they loved me and forgave me. Was this how their parents raised them, and will I be as loving with my own children? I wonder how bad they were as kids.

My life changed on July 10, 1981. I became a different person. The physical injuries and the psychological trauma I underwent transformed who I was, but my life changed because I accepted Jesus into it. The seeds my parents had sown in my life as a child sprouted and took root. My faith grew in the years that ensued.

I never arrived at my end goal of complete recovery, but the reason was not that I quit. There came a time when I realized there was no going back to being the person I once was, physically nor in any other aspect of life. Although my original goal was to continue rehab until I could run as fast and jump as high and lift as much weight, and complete trigonometry, I was awakened to the truth one day that those achievements were no longer important because I was on a different path of life, a path with new meaning and purpose and one of deeper understanding of what really mattered in life.

Every year near the anniversary date of the accident, however, I would find myself cast into a deep spell of depression. As if a depression bomb fell out of the sky and struck me atop my head, I'd re-experience the trauma. Recurrent and intrusive recollections of the event in the form of intense psychological distress associated with the physical pain and mental anguish caused an emotional and psychic numbness and an increased tendency to want to commit suicide. Self-worth plummeted. I became hopeless, despite whatever good fortune I had in my life. I cried without knowing why, other than that I was depressed. Sucked into a vacuum of empty meaning, life, I reasoned, was not worth living anymore. One year in July as I lay in bed, unable to sleep, I analyzed my life and broke down in tears without knowing why.

"What's the matter, Mart?" Dad asked as I walked into the family room where he sat and watched television.

"I don't know, Dad. It's like something has control over me," I told him. "I'm depressed." Concerned, he searched for a reason.

"You have a roof over your head, so that couldn't be it. Mom fed us a big meal tonight, so it probably wasn't because there wasn't enough food. Unless you didn't like what she fed you tonight. Was that it?" he joked, in attempt to lighten me up.

"No," I shook my head. "I don't know what happened, but I was trying to get to sleep, when suddenly I became sad and began crying." Year after year, no matter how happy my life was or how much my physical condition had improved, I'd succumb to the post-traumatic stress attack. The next year it happened at Great America amusement park. Another year while I drove on the highway. And the next year while at work at a drugstore.

Finally, I met Fr. Jack Shea, a noted Catholic professor and author, at a conference. I took advantage of the opportunity to speak with him about my recurring stress attacks. He thought for a moment then advised me to return to the scene of the accident, spend some time there and soak up the surroundings. Don't expect anything to happen, he said, not immediately, anyway.

Nothing did happen, then, at the corner, nor the following anniversary date, nor the year after. Closure had finally occurred.

I had visited the accident site with my friend Ray Norkus. I was afraid to go there alone, unsure of what might happen to me. Would I have a sudden flashback and re-experience the accident? Maybe I would arrive at the corner, look around and pass out. Although Fr. Shea said I would not experience anything, I feared the possibility that something would happen. When we arrived at the corner, which according to the police report I veered around then collided with the oncoming jeep, I looked down the road from where the jeep came. A bit curved, so she probably didn't even see me. It happened so suddenly. In a moment's time. If I had turned the corner a second or two earlier or later, maybe my life wouldn't have changed.

◆　　　◆　　　◆

I've spent very little time pondering the great, "What if...?" question since the accident. Instead, I finally took a much deeper look inside and began to ask a bigger question: Who am I?

My first semester of college I picked up a book on the psychology of love and the process of self-actualization. An amazing discovery I made that evening motivated me to live to the fullest possible extent every waking minute that remained. I read that from birth to death a person is capable of becoming no more than five percent of what they are totally capable of becoming. And most people don't even attain five percent.

Henry David Thoreau is quoted, "Oh, God, to have reached the point of death only to find out that you have never lived at all."

I have the potential to become whatever I want. I can. You can. Anyone can. So, I try. I fell short of my goal many times. Didn't finish the first 20-km race I ran after the accident. Wasn't accepted at the University of Alabama graduate school. Several publishing companies rejected my manuscripts. Turned down for several jobs. My first fiancée never married me. I never broke my personal-best 10-km time. But I didn't quit. I got up and tried again because I believed, despite what others said about how slim the odds might have been. I would set my goal, turn on my cassette tape of positive message songs and tape up on my walls signs of smiley faces, arrows pointing upward, plus signs, YES signs, thumbs-up signs.

And eventually I ran and completed a 20-km race, twice; my best time was 1:36.18, a 7:45 mile average. I completed a master's degree at Loyola University Chicago's Institute of Pastoral Studies. Cardinal Bernadin called me on the telephone and told me he had appointed two of his associates to seek college scholarship money for me. I skydived out of an airplane 3,000 feet in the air.

One of the world's largest writer's agencies in New York advised me to rewrite parts of my first novel, *On the Edge of Darkness,* so they could then market it to publishing companies. I published thousands of articles in newspapers and magazines. I self-published my own books. I fell in love and married a beautiful woman. We have a baby girl, Katie. All this and so much more! Like travels to Ireland, Austria, Germany, and Jamaica, and ministry in the Appalachian Mountains, the inner city of Chicago, and the cornfields of Kansas. Self-discovery and inner healing through 12-step groups and personal counselors and self-help psychology and love books. Still more, because life doesn't run out of itself. There will be more, as sure as there are more people to lead us to more life, and that life, I firmly believe, comes through faith in God.

◆　　◆　　◆

Journaling became a nighttime ritual of mine ever since January 1, 1981. As I've looked back through some 3,700 pages, I came to realize that more than anything I've done or any place I've visited, what's most important to me in life is people. All the people who make an impression upon my heart, who walk with me through life for however long a time, who help influence my decisions, who in some way reach out and care. Each and every person's name is logged in my journal. Hundreds upon hundreds of names, listed in the first few volumes. The list has multiplied. Currently I am in volume 16.

My past has and always will remain an important part of my life, not so much that I live in the past or dwell on old memories, rather I remain connected to all those with whom I have shared life's journey. They will always be with me, permanently, in my journal, my mind, and my heart. The past never leaves us. Some of us may try and leave the past behind, or try and forget the painful memories it holds. I have met several men and women in 12-step programs who embody excruciatingly painful childhood experiences. They realize that they cannot escape the past, only heal from it.

Others of us with less painful childhoods treasure more of its fond moments. We, all of us, are who we are because of our past. Where we stand here and now is because of the decisions we have made and the turns we have taken. Hopefully, the majority of those memories are joyful and overshadow the dark ones.

Paul writes in his letter to the Corinthians, "For the body itself is not made up of one part, but of many parts.... All of you, then, is Christ's body, and each one is a part of it" (1Corinthians 12:14, 27). One cannot do without the other.

Many people brought God's presence to me and showed me His love. Many others allowed me to bring God's love to them. For all this I am grateful. One of my first calls to ministry occurred shortly before I graduated with a bachelor's degree in journalism from SIU-Carbondale. Through months of discernment, I realized my calling was not immediately to the field of newspaper reporting, but to serve as a lay minister volunteer in Kansas. Whereas I believed I had been called to serve the people of the rural farm towns for nine months, the exact opposite happened upon several occasions. They'd served me. While driving home down a dark, unlit dirt road after

3 in the morning, my fuel gauge fell below the "E." I was 17 miles from home. I knew that any moment the car would stop and I'd be stranded in the middle of a corn-field with no all-night gas stations in sight. Besides acres of corn, the only other sight was a farmhouse. My only chance of making it home that night depended on the slight chance that the man inside the farmhouse, first of all, wouldn't pull out his shotgun when he heard a knock on the door. Then, that he'd be sympathetic with my plight. And lastly, that he would have a can of gasoline in the barn and allow me to use some of it to get home. Odds were slim. Every cell in my body prayed to God.

As I walked to the front door, a Labrador howled and barked to alert his master. I watched and waited for the rifle to be pointed my direction. Slowly, I approached the door and knocked. A tall, slender man opened the door. I explained to him that I had come from Chicago to work as a lay minister volunteer in Kansas and that my car was near empty and needed some gas to make it home to Onaga.

"Sure, I can help you. My brother owns the gas sta-tion in town, so let me go in and call him. He'd be glad to open up and fill your tank."

I mumbled under my breath...*but it's 3 o'clock in the morning, and I woke you up, and I'm a stranger, from Chicago, you know, where all the gangsters are?*

None of that mattered. The farmer's brother filled the car up. I arrived home safely. Thanks, God.

Another incident occurred about the same time in the morning a few months later. As I drove along the highway in the rain, I noticed a man walking alongside the road. Where is he going at this time of night? There's nothing out here. Mother's messages from childhood played in my head. *"Don't ever pick up any hitchhikers under any circumstances whatsoever. Do you understand me?"*

As a child I did understand, Mom, but now I'm an adult.

I slowed down as my car approached the young man. I rolled down the window and asked if he needed a lift.

"I can't thank you enough," he began as he sat down in the passenger seat. "I've been walking since I got out of court today and I'm trying to get home."

"I got out of court" resounded in my head. What was he doing in court? Trial for murder, drugs, or rape? Should I have heeded Mom's advice? Lord, You are with me, aren't You?

"You see, I lost my job last week, then my wife filed for a divorce, then on top of that I lost my driver's license because I was drinking and driving," he said. "But ever since I left the courthouse, good things have been happening. I think my life is starting to turn around. I got a ride to the county line from a policeman back there, and he tried to contact another policeman in the next county to give me a ride through, but I guess he didn't get hold of anyone, so I just started walking, then you come along and offer me a ride. Listen, you can just drop me off wherever you have to turn off the main road and I can walk the rest of the way," he said, thankful for the ride.

I drove the man home, grateful for the opportunity I was given to help a stranger in need. Before he got out of the car, he expressed interest in going to church and getting to know God. I continued to pray for him.

I imagine sometimes that when I enter the gates of heaven and look to see the face of God, I will instead see the faces of hundreds and thousands of people who made God present to me in my life. Truly, I will not be disappointed. Without people, I have learned, life can become lonely, empty and less meaningful. Without people, less life.

◆　　　◆　　　◆

In the years following my recovery and after I earned my bachelor's degree, I'd often find myself reflecting on life. "I never thought I'd be where I am now, doing what I'm doing." Sometimes I would be seated at a bar having a beer wondering why I was still single, living at home, working three jobs to make ends meet and struggling to pay off college loans, instead of employed and experiencing fulfillment in a career field of my liking and driving a classy sports car home to my family's two-story house with an in-ground swimming pool. After all, my life was destined for happiness and success as a newspaper reporter ever since sixth grade when I received a certificate from the governor for an essay I wrote. From there on out, writing was my life. I was destined for a life as a reporter. The road was straight, paved, and marked with signposts pointing towards the newspaper field. Then, God appeared.

During a homily at Mass, a priest once said, in reference to placing one's trust in God and living a life filled with faith, "Do you want to know how to make God laugh?

Tell God your plans for your future." I once had plans. God entered my life and changed those plans. It's made all the difference.

◆　　　◆　　　◆

I'm 16 years older. I've worked in the field of ministry as a volunteer or staff member since 1983. Yet the longer I live and the more I learn, the less I realize I really know. Perhaps two of the most valuable lessons I've learned through all of this are the simplest: I need God, and it doesn't take knowledge or education to help people—the sick, infirm, dying, families in farm crises, handicapped. All we need to do is reach out and connect. Listen to one another. Embrace and comfort someone. We can all do it. We are the body of Christ.

About the Author

Marty Folan graduated from Southern Illinois University at Carbondale, with a B.S. in journalism and minors in religion and community development. He earned two scholarships for his writing. His achievements and activities, since his accident, include running 20 km. (12.4 miles) races, skydiving, ministry work, and his involvement in the Knights of Columbus.

After college graduation, he joined a lay ministry volunteer organization in Kansas, where he lived with a priest and served as a youth and family minister.

He completed a master's degree in Pastoral Studies at the Institute of Pastoral Studies at Loyola University Chicago in 1994.

Currently, he is writing and working as Youth Ministry Coordinator at St. George Parish in Tinley Park, IL. Happily married, he lives with his wife Jeannine and their new baby, Katie, in Joliet.